BACKSLIDING

Backsliding
Understanding Weakness of Will

ALFRED R. MELE

UNIVERSITY PRESS

Oxford University Press is a department of the University of Oxford.
It furthers the University's objective of excellence in research, scholarship,
and education by publishing worldwide.

Oxford   New York
Auckland   Cape Town   Dar es Salaam   Hong Kong   Karachi
Kuala Lumpur   Madrid   Melbourne   Mexico City   Nairobi
New Delhi   Shanghai   Taipei   Toronto

With offices in
Argentina   Austria   Brazil   Chile   Czech Republic   France   Greece
Guatemala   Hungary   Italy   Japan   Poland   Portugal   Singapore
South Korea   Switzerland   Thailand   Turkey   Ukraine   Vietnam

Oxford is a registered trade mark of Oxford University Press
in the UK and certain other countries.

Published in the United States of America by
Oxford University Press
198 Madison Avenue, New York, NY 10016

© Oxford University Press 2012

First issued as an Oxford University Press paperback, 2014.

All rights reserved. No part of this publication may be reproduced, stored in a retrieval system,
or transmitted, in any form or by any means, without the prior permission in writing of
Oxford University Press, or as expressly permitted by law, by license, or under terms agreed
with the appropriate reproduction rights organization. Inquiries concerning reproduction
outside the scope of the above should be sent to the Rights Department,
Oxford University Press, at the address above.

You must not circulate this work in any other form
and you must impose this same condition on any acquirer.

Library of Congress Cataloging-in-Publication Data
Mele, Alfred R., 1951–
Backsliding : understanding weakness of will / Alfred R. Mele.
p. cm.
Includes bibliographical references (p.) and index.
ISBN 978-0-19-989613-4 (hardcover : alk. paper); 978-0-19-936664-4 (paperback : alk. paper)
1. Akrasia. I. Title.
BJ1468.5.M45 2012
128'.3—dc23   2011030339

For my mother's sisters: Elizabeth, Lucy, Lydia, and Mary

Contents

Preface	ix
1. Introduction	1
2. Weakness of Will and Akrasia	13
3. Weakness and Compulsion	33
4. Accounting for Backsliding: Background and More	57
5. Self-Control	91
6. Conclusion	115
Notes	123
References	133
Index	141

Preface

"Backsliding" is the title of R. M. Hare's chapter on what he calls moral weakness in *Freedom and Reason* (Hare 1963). I use the term here to gesture at phenomena associated with what is sometimes called weakness of will. Much of my first book, *Irrationality* (Mele 1987), was on weakness of will. I take another shot at the topic here—a quarter of a century later. In my view, backsliding is a very real phenomenon. If many people did not share this opinion of mine, self-help books would not sell nearly as well as they do. My primary aim in this book is to improve our understanding of why we backslide.

Portions of this book derive from some of my published articles. Chapter 2 is an updated version of Mele 2010b, parts of chapter 3 are based on Mele 2002a, and chapter 5 incorporates material from Mele 2011. I also draw on some of my previous books—especially Mele 1987 and 1995 (both of which explore weakness of will at some length), but also Mele 2003, 2006a, and 2009.

Some of the material in this book was presented at SUNY-Stony Brook, Tilburg University, the University of Birmingham Law School, and Utrecht University. I am grateful to my audiences for their feedback. For additional feedback, I am grateful to students in seminar discussions of a draft of this book at Florida State University, Richard Holton, Stephen Kearns, and anonymous referees.

This book was made possible through the support of a grant from the John Templeton Foundation. The opinions expressed in this publication are my own and do not necessarily reflect the views of the John Templeton Foundation.

BACKSLIDING

ONE

• • •

Introduction

Alexandra Logue opens her *Self-Control* with the following sentence: "People often do things that result in some immediate gratification, but which in the long run are not very beneficial" (1995, p. 3). The examples she offers include smoking cigarettes, having unprotected sex, and going to a party rather than studying for a test. Sometimes, when people do these things, they act *contrary to their better judgment*— or so, at least, it seems. In many such cases, it also seems true that these people are not moved by irresistible desires to perform the intentional actions that clash with their better judgments, are neither insane nor severely depressed, and act freely. If and when this actually happens—as opposed to merely seeming to happen—people act in a weak-willed way, as such action is traditionally conceived.

Some philosophers have argued that things are not as they seem in this domain. In Plato's *Protagoras* (352b–358d), Socrates rejects the popular belief that sometimes "people who know what it is best to do are not willing to do it, though it is in their power, but do something else" (352d). Plato's own (or later) position does not differ importantly from the Socratic one for my purposes. Although Plato accepts the possibility of acting contrary to one's better judgment (*Republic* 439e–440b; *Laws* 689a–b, 863a–e), he embraces Socrates's thesis that, when this happens, doing what one knew to be best was not in one's power (*Laws* 860c–863e). The idea, on one interpretation, is that what seems to be weak-willed action is actually unfree action.[1]

1

This idea is not restricted to the ancient world. Versions of it are defended by R. M. Hare (1963, ch. 5), Gary Watson (1977), and David Pugmire (1982), among others. Hare appeals to an alleged logical connection between judgment and action (1963, p. 79) whereas Watson and Pugmire focus on the notion of resistance, contending that any agent who could have successfully resisted temptation would have done so. I examine their arguments in *Irrationality* (1987, ch. 2), and I return to some of them in chapter 3.

About half of *Irrationality* is devoted to weak-willed action. I try to show there that such action is possible and to explain why it happens. Not everyone has been persuaded, and I try again in this book (while also trying to avoid excessive repetition).[2]

When I wrote *Irrationality*, the word "will" in such expressions as "weakness of will" and "free will" made me uneasy. It can conjure up the supernatural in the minds of some readers, and I definitely did not want to do that. In that book, for stylistic reasons, I used the classical Greek term "akrasia" much more often than "weakness of will" (one of its translations), and I wrote in terms of akratic action rather than weak-willed action. This is more difficult to do now than it was then because Richard Holton subsequently argued that people can exhibit akrasia without exhibiting weakness of will and vice versa (1999, 2009, ch. 4). (I examine Holton's position in chapter 2.) In the present chapter, I use "akrasia" and "akratic" in setting part of the stage, but eventually the expressions "weakness of will" and "weak-willed" displace their counterparts (for reasons that emerge in chapter 2). When I use these expressions, I definitely have nothing supernatural in mind.

1. Background

The present section provides terminological and conceptual background, including a description of a central species of akratic action. Whether any actions have all of the features identified in that description is a topic for subsequent chapters.

What Aristotle called akrasia is, very roughly, a trait of character exhibited in uncompelled intentional behavior that is contrary to the agent's better judgment. What he called enkrateia (self-control, continence, strength of will) is, again roughly, a trait of character exhibited in behavior that conforms with the agent's better judgment in the face of temptation to act to the contrary. The akratic person, Aristotle writes, "is in such a state as to be defeated even by those [pleasures] which most people master," and the enkratic person is in such a state as "to master even those by which most people are defeated" (*Nicomachean Ethics* 1150a11–13).

Aristotle limits the sphere of enkrateia and akrasia, like that of temperance and self-indulgence (*Nicomachean Ethics* 3.10, 7.7), to "pleasures and pains and appetites and aversions arising through touch and taste" (1150a9–10).[3] However, self-control and akrasia have come to be understood much more broadly. Self-control, as it is now conceived, may be exhibited in the successful resistance of actual or anticipated temptation in any sphere. Temptations having to do with sexual activity, eating, drinking, smoking, and the like are tied to touch and taste. But people also are tempted to work less or more than they judge best, to gamble beyond the limits they have set for themselves, to spend more or less on gifts than they believe they should, and so on. Apparently, we can exercise self-control in overcoming such temptations or akratically succumb to them.

There is a middle ground between akrasia and enkrateia— the character traits—and there is no requirement that all akratic actions manifest akrasia. Suppose that Ann, who is more self-controlled than most people in general and regarding alcohol consumption in particular, freely succumbs to temptation in that sphere contrary to her better judgment in a particularly trying situation. Even though she does not exhibit akrasia, as Aristotle represents that trait, she may exhibit an associated imperfection—imperfect self-control—in an akratic action. Similarly, a person with the trait of akrasia may occasionally succeed in resisting temptation and act in a self-controlled way. In the recent philosophical literature, akratic and enkratic *actions* have received considerably more attention than the character traits. In this book, I follow suit. (A theorist may choose to use the expression "weakness of will" to name a trait of character, as Aristotle used "akrasia" to name one. To forestall potential confusion, I report that I myself do not so choose. As I use the expression, Ann may exhibit weakness of will in the example I presented even though she lacks the character trait in question.)

I have argued elsewhere (Mele 1987, 1995) that not all akratic actions are contrary to the agent's better judgment. (I return to this issue in chapter 2.) The (alleged) akratic actions that concern me in the present section *are* contrary to such judgments. One feature of these judgments, as I conceive of them (following an ancient tradition), is that their contents are declarative propositions—propositions that may be either true or false.[4] Another feature is that they are based on the agent's own values and beliefs (or what he takes to be his values and beliefs). The literature on akratic action is *not* focused, for example, on the question how an agent can freely and intentionally A even though he judges that, from the evaluative perspective of his elders (or his peers), it is best not to A. It is the agent's evaluative perspective that is featured. This is a start.

The better judgments at issue require further attention. Some of what I am about to say about such judgments is a bit technical. The technicality is the price to be paid for avoiding confusion.

Donald Davidson defines akratic action as follows:

> D. In doing x an agent acts incontinently if and only if: (a) the agent does x intentionally; (b) the agent believes that there is an alternative action y open to him; and (c) the agent judges

that, all things considered, it would be better to do *y* than to do *x*. (1980, p. 22)

A technical problem with this definition is easily spotted. Alf satisfies all three conditions; but although he judges that, all things considered, it would be better to do *y* than to do *x*, he also judges that, all things considered, it would be better to do *x* and *z* than to do *y*. Alf intentionally does *x* and *z* in accordance with the latter better judgment, and he does not do *y*. Other things being equal, he does not act akratically despite satisfying Davidson's three conditions. (I offer readers who would like a concrete example the following one. Alf judges it better to run a mile before breakfast today than to ride a bike for a mile before breakfast, but he also judges it better to ride a bike for a mile and swim a mile before breakfast than to run a mile before breakfast. Alf intentionally both rides a bike for a mile and swims a mile before breakfast today; and he does not run a mile before breakfast.)

This problem is solved by defining judgment-violating akratic action in terms of a judgment to the effect that it would be *best* to A. (Notice that Alf might have judged that, all things considered, it would be best to *x* and *z*.) In instances of judgment-violating akratic action, agents do not need to judge that a course of action A is the best of all possible courses of action. They may judge that A is better than the alternatives they have envisioned—that it is the best of the envisioned options, and best not just in some qualified respect or other, but on the whole. If, even so, they do not A and they instead freely and intentionally pursue one of the envisioned alternatives in the absence of insanity and severe depression, they act akratically.

There is a potential technical problem with defining judgment-violating akratic action in terms of a judgment that it is best to A. If "best" is used exclusively, the definition might not cover all possible cases of judgment-violating akratic action. Perhaps an agent who judges that two different courses of action, *A* and *B*, are tied for the top spot may akratically do something else, *C*. Perhaps the same is true of an agent who regards *A* and *B* as incommensurable and judges that each of them is superior to the other alternatives. A way around the problem is provided by the possibility of negative best judgments of a certain kind. The agent in either of the scenarios just sketched may judge (in effect) that it would be best on the whole *not to do* anything incompatible with his doing *A* or *B*; and if akratic action is possible, he may act akratically in doing *C*. An inclusive reading of "best" generates its own problem. When "best" is used inclusively, an agent's judgment that *A* and *B* are tied for the top spot counts as a judgment that each of *A* and *B* is best. If *A* and *B* are mutually exclusive and the agent *B*-s, he may be said to act contrary to his judgment that *A* is best, but he presumably does not act akratically. I opt for the exclusive reading of "best."

I asked about the nature of the better judgment involved in judgment-violating akratic action, and I offered an answer. Setting aside ties for first place and incommensurability, it is a judgment to the effect that it is best on the whole to *A*, "best" being understood exclusively and as relativized to options envisioned by the agent; the content of the judgment may be either true or false; and the judgment is based on the agent's own values and beliefs (or what he takes to be his values and beliefs). Henceforth, this is what I mean by "better judgment" (when ties for first place and incommensurability are not at issue). When I say that someone judges it best to *A*, it should not be inferred that he judges that *A* is the best of all possible courses of action, and "best" should be understood as shorthand for "best on the whole."

Some sentences attributing better judgments to agents are ambiguous. A philosopher who writes "Carl judged it best to *A*" may or may not mean that Carl made a judgment that it is best to *A*, where to make a judgment is to make a cognitive decision—to decide that it is best to *A*. Someone's *making a judgment*, as I understand the expression, is an event. But the author of the sentence about Carl may mean only that Carl believed that it was best to *A*; and Carl's believing this is not an event. Some beliefs that it is best to *A* may be acquired without any explicit reasoning. When Donna's sister phoned to say that their father had suffered a serious heart attack and might not live much longer, it was obvious to Donna that it would be best to get to the hospital as soon as possible. Though she was aware of other options, she did not deliberate about which option was best. The expression "better judgment" in philosophical discussions of akratic action is at least suggestive of a belief arrived at on the basis of conscious deliberation. But I do not make acting against a belief so arrived at a necessary condition of judgment-violating akratic action.

Two kinds of scenario should be distinguished. In one kind, agents act contrary to better judgments they made some time ago, did not revise, and are not aware of now. In a second kind, agents are aware of the better judgments they are acting against. I discuss each kind of scenario in turn.

Here is a scenario of the first kind. A day after she barely avoided disaster while driving home under the influence of alcohol, Beth judged it best never again to drive while over the legal limit for alcohol. Three weeks later, after having a few drinks with friends at a bar, she considers asking a friend for a ride home but is put off by thoughts of how inconvenient it would be to retrieve her car from the bar's parking lot the following morning. Beth believes that she probably has had too much to drink to drive home legally. But she decides to drive home anyway (and fortunately manages to get there safely). She does not recall the judgment she made three weeks ago; nor does she consciously believe that it would be best not to drive tonight.

Perhaps Beth exhibits some weakness of will in this story. It may be argued, for example, that she exhibits it in allowing her thoughts about inconvenience to play the role they played in generating her decision to drive home. In the absence of any weakness of will, it may be claimed, Beth would have come to the conclusion that it was best not to drive home and would have decided and acted accordingly. I leave this open now. My present aim is to distinguish stories like Beth's from stories of another kind.

Beth acts contrary to a better judgment that she once made. She did not revise it. But she does not consciously remember it either. Alleged cases of akratic action that receive the bulk of the attention in the literature are different: in them, agents are aware at the time of action that they are acting contrary to their better judgment. Furthermore, the judgments are based on practical reasoning.[5] It will be useful to have a label for akratic action of this kind. I call it *core akratic action* and define it as free, sane, intentional action that, as the nondepressed agent consciously recognizes at the time of action, is contrary to his better judgment, a judgment based on practical reasoning.[6]

The references to sanity and depression in the definition just offered require some attention. I start with the former. That akratic actions do not manifest insanity is typically taken for granted but rarely made explicit. Consider the following case (from Mele 2002b, p. 213). Ike is at home thinking about whether to attend a friend's party or go to a ball game instead. He regards these options as far superior to the alternatives that have come to mind, but he is unsure about which is better. As Ike is thinking about this, it strikes him that he might remove his clothes, don a cowboy hat, and twirl his son's toy six-guns while riding the subway to an amusement park. Although Ike deems this inferior to the options he had been considering, this is what he decides to do. And he acts accordingly—until the police carry him away. An intuitive reaction to this case is that even if Ike is not compelled to decide and act as he does, his problem is not weakness of will but (perhaps temporary) insanity. Incidentally, the thought of substituting his son's Martian mask and ray gun for the cowboy gear flashed through Ike's mind, and he could have decided to do that and executed that decision.

Theorists who hold that no actions that manifest insanity are free actions can say that Ike does not perform any akratic actions in this story because the actions at issue are not free. But not all philosophers who write about free will endorse a sanity requirement on free action; and some seem to take positions on free action that commit them to regarding some actions that manifest insanity as free (on this, see Mele 2006a, pp. 78–79, n. 7, and p. 80, n. 19). They may find a sanity requirement on akratic action useful.

I turn to depression. Philosophers have argued about whether agents' beliefs that they themselves ought, morally, to *A* necessarily encompass motivation to *A*. I have argued elsewhere (Mele 1996a; 2003, ch. 5) that no plausible moral theory will entail that first-person moral ought beliefs (understood as attitudes with truth-valued content) necessarily encompass motivation to act accordingly. Part of the argument involves a story about listlessness, something akin to clinical depression. In that story, because of the deaths of her husband and children in a plane crash last night, Eve lost all motivation to continue aiding her ailing uncle even though she continued to believe that she morally ought to help him, as she had regularly been doing before the crash. I argued for the conceptual possibility of the story. If that argument succeeds, it also is conceptually possible for Eve to believe that it would be *best* to help her uncle today while having no motivation to help him. Suppose she knows that her uncle needs her help most in the mornings and she believes that it would be best to help him this morning. But although Eve has some motivation to do very undemanding things this morning—for example, lie in bed, sit on the couch, and walk to the bathroom—she has no motivation at all to help her uncle. So, of course, she does not help him. Now, as many philosophers understand free action, Eve's listlessness is compatible with her performing free actions that morning—for example, freely lying in bed, freely lying on the couch, freely walking to the bathroom. If they are right, the requirement that akratic actions be free actions does not block the possibility that Eve acts akratically. However, even if Eve is freely doing these things while not doing what she believes it best to do, one may be excused for thinking that she is not exhibiting weakness of will and instead is manifesting a much more severe problem.

Some readers may be inclined to think that Eve is exhibiting weakness of will—and therefore acting akratically—on the grounds that if her will were stronger, she would beat back the effects of depression, drive to her uncle's house, and help him, as she believes best. I have no wish to argue about this. My concern now is with central cases of akratic action, and they do not include listlessness. I do not claim that depressed agents cannot act akratically, but I also do not claim that all akratic actions are *core* akratic actions.

Brief comments on two additional topics are in order before I close this section. In paradigmatic cases of akratic action, the judgment that the agent acts against is rationally made and rationally held. However, I do not see rationality in these connections as a requirement for akratic action, and I do not make it a necessary condition for core akratic action. Owing partly to an irrational overestimation of his abilities, a person may judge it best to attempt a dangerous feat—for example, diving into a lake from a high cliff. Even if the judgment is irrational, he may act akratically in backing away from the cliff. Rationally reassessing matters is one thing; acting contrary to one's better judgment owing to a controllable fear is another.

A technical issue about action merits attention here because of its bearing on how the notion of akratic conduct is to be articulated. There may be cases in which even though it is intentional on a person's part that he does not A, his not A-ing is not an action and therefore is not an intentional action. An ordinary case in which a person intentionally does not vote in an election may be a case in point (Mele 2003, pp. 151–53). If the person judges it best to vote in this election, his not voting may be akratic even if it is not an action.

2. Preview

I conclude the present chapter with a preview of the remaining five. Some readers like to know where they are heading. I am happy to oblige.

There is a voluminous philosophical literature that at least purports to be about weakness of will. Richard Holton has developed a view of the nature of weak-willed actions that, as he reports, departs "from almost all of the literature on the subject" (1999, p. 242). If his view is correct, much of what has been written about akrasia and akratic actions is not about weakness of will and weak-willed actions. In chapter 2, I argue that my view of the nature of akratic actions, as articulated in *Irrationality* and elsewhere, fares considerably better in the sphere of weakness of will than Holton's view does. The chapter's aim is to clarify the nature of weak-willed actions.

Some readers may worry that until we know how alleged weak-willed actions differ from unfree actions contrary to the agent's better judgment, we should not believe that weak-willed actions occur. In chapter 3, I argue that this worry is seriously inflated. I show that the leading arguments for the thesis that no actions that conflict with our better judgments can be free are unpersuasive, I identify significant problems that any philosopher who endeavors to defend that thesis will encounter, and I sketch various ways of distinguishing between unfree actions contrary to one's better judgment and weak-willed actions.

At the beginning of chapter 3, the expression "core weak-willed action" replaces "core akratic action." In chapter 4, I sketch a theoretical and empirical framework that sheds light on how the occurrence of core weak-willed actions may be accounted for *if* they occur, and I apply that framework to an apparent case of core weak-willed action. Toward the end of the chapter I raise a question about the agent's prospects for a successful exercise of self-control in that case.

Self-control is the topic of chapter 5. In the first four sections, I discuss work on self-control in a trio of fields: philosophy, psychiatry, and social psychology. I then take up the question whether agents who fail to make a successful effort of self-control in the service of their conscious better judgments could ever have done otherwise, and I argue for an affirmative answer.

Chapter 6 is a brief conclusion. There I explain why readers who believe that we often act freely are in a position to conclude that core weak-willed actions are not only psychologically possible but actual as well.

TWO

• • •

Weakness of Will and Akrasia

Philosophical work on weakness of will in various modern languages is heavily influenced by Plato's and Aristotle's work on akrasia. Often, philosophers who write on the topic in English are much less concerned to capture ordinary usage of the expression "weakness of will" than to capture the meaning of "akrasia" (translations include "incontinence," "want of self-control," and "weakness of will"); and when they turn their attention to conceptual or psychological possibility or impossibility, it tends to be akratic action that they focus on. Richard Holton is an exception.[1] He aims to "give an account of our ordinary notion of weakness of will" (1999, p. 262), and he views that notion as distinct from the notion of akrasia (pp. 243, 255).[2]

In *Irrationality* (1987), I develop a view of the nature of akratic action. (I do this to prepare the way for the construction and defense of a theory about why a central species of akratic action is conceptually and psychologically possible.) How well does that view fare in the sphere of weakness of will? Considerably better than Holton's account. That is a thesis of this chapter. My aim is to clarify the nature of weakness of will.

Holton reports that he is "trying to give an account of our ordinary notion of weakness of will" (1999, p. 262). One way to get evidence about ordinary notions is to survey ordinary people (that is, people who are not specialists on the topic). In this connection, I conducted five survey studies on weakness of will. The results are reported in section 2, where Holton's account of weakness of will and support he offers for it are examined. Section 1 presents a sketch of my view of the nature of akratic action. Section 3 wraps things up.

1. Akrasia and Akratic Action

In the present section, I write in terms of akratic and enkratic action to signal that I am working with traditional conceptions of the apparent phenomena. In section 2, where I take up Holton's account of weakness of will, I switch to ordinary English.

In *Irrationality*, I focus on what I call *strict* akratic action. It is similar to what I call *core* akratic action in chapter 1—free, sane, intentional action that, as the nondepressed agent consciously recognizes at the time of action, is contrary to his better judgment, a judgment based on practical reasoning. (The differences between the definitions owe to some fine-tuning.)

One feature that core akratic actions share with all akratic actions, as traditionally conceived, is that they are contrary to the agent's better judgment.[3] However, I suggest in *Irrationality* that "the traditional conception should be broadened to accommodate" some cases in which agents do not act contrary to their better judgment and, in fact, act in accordance with such a judgment (p. 7; see Jackson 1984, p. 4). Here is an example that motivates that suggestion:

> Rocky, who has promised his mother that he would never play tackle football, has just been invited by some older boys to play in tomorrow's pick-up game. He believes that his promise evaluatively defeats his reasons for playing and consequently judges that it would be best not to play; but he decides to play anyway. However, when the time comes, he suffers a failure of nerve. He does not show up for the game—not because he judges it best not to play, but rather because he is afraid. He would not have played even if he had . . . judged it best to do so. (1987, p. 7)

I claimed that "Rocky's failure to play in the football game may exhibit weakness of will even though he judges it best not to play" (p. 7). (I was using "weakness of will" interchangeably with "akrasia.")

A theorist who grants that Rocky akratically refrains from playing may be inclined to believe that there is no place for evaluative judgment in a proper analysis of akratic action and that traditional conceptions of akratic action should be radically revised. I have argued (1992b, 1995, ch. 4) against radical revision and for conceptions of akratic action and its contrary that feature two different kinds of practical commitment. Attention to a story with various possible endings sets part of the stage for these conceptions:

> Young Bruce has decided to join some wayward Cub Scouts in breaking into a neighbor's house, even though he . . . judges it best not to do so. Suppose that at the last minute Bruce refuses to enter the house and leaves the scene of the crime. His doing so because his . . . judgment has prevailed is one thing; his refusing to break in owing simply to a failure of nerve is another. In the latter event, Bruce arguably has exhibited weakness of will: he "chickened out," as children are wont to exclaim.
>
> Suppose alternatively that, experiencing some trepidation about the house-breaking, Bruce tries to steel himself for the deed. Although he judges it best not to participate in the crime, he attempts, successfully, to master his fear, and he proceeds to pick the lock. Here, it seems, Bruce has exhibited strength of will; he has exercised self-control in conquering his fear. If that is right, he has done so even if—as we may suppose—he did not judge it best to master the fear that he experienced, nor judge it better to do so than not to do so. Some exercises of self-control apparently are not performed in the service of a better or best judgment. (Mele 1995, p. 60; see Mele 1987, p. 54)

Traditional conceptions of akratic action and its contrary, as I observed, "revolve around a certain species of *commitment* to action—the sort of commitment constituted by a . . . better . . .

judgment. An agent who ... judges it best to *A* is thereby *rationally committed* to *A*-ing, in the sense that (as long as the judgment is retained) the uncompelled, intentional performance of any action that he believes to be incompatible with his *A*-ing would open him to the charge of irrationality" (1995, p. 71). An uncompelled intentional action of this kind, I claimed, "would be at least *subjectively* irrational—irrational from the agent's own point of view. For, while explicitly holding the judgment, an agent cannot rationally take himself to have, from his own point of view, better (or equally good, 'best' being understood exclusively) grounds for not *A*-ing" (p. 71).

I claimed that Bruce, in my story, has both a commitment of the kind just described and a commitment of another kind—one generated by his *deciding* to break into the house (Mele 1995, p. 71). I called the two kinds of practical commitment *evaluative* and *executive*. A conception of akratic action that accommodates both akratic action as traditionally conceived and Bruce's akratically refraining from participating in the crime can be framed in terms of these two species of practical commitment. In both kinds of case, "a practical commitment is thwarted by noncompelling competing motivation" (p. 74). In traditional akratic action, the commitment is an evaluative one. In unorthodox akratic action like Bruce's, it is an executive one. I hastened to add that the thwarting of an executive commitment by noncompelling competing motivation is not conceptually sufficient for the agent's having acted akratically. As I explained,

> If, owing appropriately to his evaluative commitment and to associated desires of his, Bruce had abandoned his intention to break into the house and acted on the basis of his better judgment, he would not have acted akratically in refraining from breaking in. In unorthodox ... akratic action, the thwarting or overturning of an akratic decision or intention has *another* source—for example, controllable fear. The agent abandons his akratic intention and does the (subjectively) right thing, but not for the (subjectively) right reason. (1995, p. 74)

A conception of the contrary of akratic action—enkratic action—can also be framed in terms of the two kinds of practical commitment. In orthodox enkratic action, the agent acts on the basis of an evaluative commitment in the face of temptation. In unorthodox enkratic action, the agent lacks an evaluative commitment to *A*-ing and has an executive commitment to *A*-ing, and the decision or intention to *A* that constitutes that commitment prevails against a threat (or threats) of being undermined in such a way that if the decision or intention had been undermined in that way, the agent's refraining from *A*-ing would have been an unorthodox akratic refraining (Mele 1995, pp. 74–75).

I did not offer full-blown analyses of akratic and enkratic action. Instead, I offered sketches of conceptions of both kinds of action designed to accommodate traditional and nontraditional species of them. If these sketches were offered as sketches of *weak-willed* and *self-controlled* action, would they be hopelessly flawed? That is a question for section 2. I should add that my primary concern in my written work on akratic action has been to explain why akratic actions are psychologically possible and why they occur. My conceptual work in this sphere was undertaken in the service of the explanatory project. I offered an analysis of strict akratic action (1987, p. 7) because that is the species of akratic action I deemed most challenging from an explanatory point of view: the analysis specified the phenomenon to be explained. I had no need for an analysis of "*S* akratically *A*-s."

2. Weakness of Will

Richard Holton reports that his approach to weakness of will departs "from almost all of the literature on the subject" (1999, p. 242). In his view, "weakness of will arises ... when agents are too ready to reconsider their intentions," and he develops "the idea that the central cases of weakness of will are best characterized not as cases in which people act against their better judgment, but as cases in which they fail to act on their intentions" (p. 241; see McIntyre 2006). In the present section, I assess some of the support he offers for preferring his "account of weakness of will to the traditional account that understands weakness of will as a failure to do what one judges to be best" (p. 251). Brief attention to Holton's conception of weakness of will sets the stage.[4]

Holton's account of weakness of will features the notion of a "contrary inclination defeating intention" (1999, p. 250). Intentions of this kind are formed "in an attempt to overcome contrary desires that one believes one will have when the time comes to act."[5] In a later article, he calls such intentions *resolutions* (2003, p. 42); I will follow him in this. Holton offers the following conjunctive necessary condition for displaying weakness of will: "To display weakness of will, an agent must have formed [a resolution] that he revises.... And his revision must have been something that, by the standards of a good intender, he should not have done" (1999, p. 259). He also offers a sufficient condition: "If someone overreadily revises [a resolution], that is weakness of will" (p. 250).

I turn to some support that Holton offers for preferring his account of weakness of will to the traditional account, starting with some anecdotal evidence. He writes: "Whenever I have asked nonphilosophers what they take weakness of will to consist in, they have made no mention of judgments about the better or worse course of action. Rather they have said things like this: weak-willed people are irresolute; they do not persist in their intentions; they are too easily deflected from the path they have chosen" (1999, p. 241). This piqued my interest. So I ran some studies.

In Study 1, I asked Holton's question. The participants were seventy-two undergraduates at Florida State University. They were in the first week of a basic philosophy course, and weakness of will was not on their course agenda. The students were presented with the following text: "What is weakness of will? Please answer this question and briefly describe one example of weakness of will." Only eleven of the students (about 15%) mentioned doing something one knew or believed one should not do—either in their answers to the general question or in their examples. But only one student (about 1.4%) mentioned doing something one chose, decided, intended, or resolved not to do in either connection.[6]

In Study 2, I switched to multiple choice. Participants were 119 undergraduates at Florida State University. They were in the second week of a basic philosophy course; again weakness of will was not on their syllabus. Half (sixty) were presented with the following questionnaire, and half (fifty-nine) were presented with a version of this questionnaire that differed from it in just one way—items A and B occurred in the reverse order:

> We're interested in what the expression "weakness of will" means to you. Please answer the following question by circling your answer.
> Which of the following descriptions of weakness of will is more accurate in your opinion?
> A. Doing something you believed or knew you shouldn't do (for example, going to a party even though you believed it would be better to stay home and study).
> B. Doing something you decided or intended not to do (for example, going to a party even though you decided to stay home and study).
> C. Neither. The descriptions are equally accurate or inaccurate.

The ordering of A and B had no significant effect. The results were as follows: 49% gave the believed/knew response; 33% gave the decided/intended response; and 18% gave the third response.

As I have mentioned, Holton says that he is "trying to give an account of our ordinary notion of weakness of will" (1999, p. 262). Studies 1 and 2 provide no indication that our ordinary notion is captured better in terms of intention or decision than in terms of knowledge or belief. In fact, the studies point the other way.

Elsewhere (Mele 2001b), I have suggested that in the sphere of folk concepts, folk judgments about cases (for example, about whether or not a particular action in a vignette is intentional) are likely to be more useful than folk judgments about related theoretical propositions (for example, the proposition that intentionally *A*-ing entails intending to *A*). Some readers who agree with me about this may be disinclined to take the results of my first two surveys seriously. To such readers I pose the following question: What should be taken *more* seriously—these results or the anecdotal evidence offered by Holton that prompted me to conduct the surveys? (Later in this section, I report the results of some studies in which nonspecialists are responding to a vignette.)

Holton presents several cases in which an agent who seems to display weakness of will does not act contrary to his better judgment but does act contrary to a decision. Some of these cases have the same structure as my story about Rocky (Mele 1987, p. 7) described in the preceding section (see Holton 1999, pp. 255–57). Recall that although Rocky judges that it would be best to decline an invitation to play tackle football, he decides to play anyway. "However, when the time comes, he suffers a failure of nerve. He does not show up for the game—not because he judges it best not to play, but rather because he is afraid" (1987, p. 7). In a parallel case that Holton presents, Christabel decides against her better judgment to "embark on an affair" (1999, p. 255). "At the very last moment, however, she pulls out: not because of a rational reconsideration of the pros and cons, but because she simply loses her nerve."

As I see it, Christabel, like Rocky, displays weakness of will. (Like Holton, I do not use the expression "weakness of will" as a label for a character trait. See note 4.) Obviously, the claim that these two agents display weakness of will is compatible both with Holton's account of weakness of will and with my view that weakness of will can be displayed both in acting contrary to an evaluative commitment and in acting contrary to an executive commitment.

Holton claims that if Christabel were to act on her decision, we would "have *akrasia* without weakness of will" (1999, p. 256). It is clear that in embarking on the affair she would be acting akratically (provided that this is not an instance of compelled action). But is it also clear that her embarking on the affair does not display weakness of will? Readers who wish to make a judgment about this should be given the remaining details that Holton provides. Christabel is "an unmarried Victorian lady" (p. 255). She "considers [the prospective affair] morally wrong," and "she knows [it] will be disastrous. It will ruin her reputation, and quite probably leave her pregnant."

Is any weakness of will displayed in the scenario in which Christabel decides to have the affair and follows through? Some readers may be inclined to judge that some weakness of will is displayed in Christabel's *deciding* as she does, and that, in the absence of any such weakness, she would have decided to act as she judged best and would have acted accordingly. A person with a stronger will, they might think, would not have succumbed to temptation. Some such readers may worry that their reaction to this story is biased by their philosophical education—that their conception of weakness of will owes too much to the work of Plato and Aristotle on akrasia or to subsequent philosophical work that purports to be about weakness of will but really is about akrasia. If the anecdotal evidence about weakness of will that Holton offers were known to be on target, then these readers really should worry that they are not good judges about, in Holton's words, "our ordinary notion of weakness of will" (1999, p. 262). But that anecdotal evidence is challenged by the studies I reported; those studies provide evidence that lay folk are more inclined to think of weakness of will in terms of doing what one knew or believed one should not do than in terms of doing something that one decided or intended not to do.

Consider a version of Christabel's story in which she masters her fear and proceeds with the affair, as she decided to do against her better judgment. Some readers may judge that she displays some strength of will in mastering her fear and acting as she decided to act. And some of the same readers may judge that she displays some weakness of will in deciding to embark on the affair against her better judgment and in embarking on it. As these readers would have it, Christabel's embarking on the affair displays both some strength of will and some weakness of will. Are they embracing a contradiction? Not as I see it. They can consistently hold both that, in the absence of any weakness of will, Christabel would not have decided to embark on the affair and would not have embarked on it and that, even so, in mastering her fear and embarking on the affair she displays some strength of will; a person with less strength of will would have caved in to the fear.[7]

Return to Holton's claim that if Christabel were to act on her decision, we would "have *akrasia* without weakness of will" (1999, p. 256). As I see it, emboldened partly by the points I have made about Holton's anecdotal evidence and the studies I reported, we would have both. I am more confident about what akrasia is than I am about "our ordinary notion of weakness of will" (Holton 1999, p. 262). But the studies I reported indicate that this ordinary notion is much closer to a relatively standard conception of akrasia than Holton would have us believe.[8]

Another alleged example of akrasia without weakness of will merits attention. Holton writes: "I have a friend who believes that all the arguments point to the same conclusion: he should not eat meat. But he is not moved. 'I am,' he says disarmingly, 'inconsistent.' . . . Although he is *akratic*, he does not attract the stigma that attaches to weakness of will. Indeed, I would never call this friend weak willed" (Holton 1999, p. 253; also see 2003, p. 41).

In an attempt to illustrate an important difference between akratic and weak-willed action, Holton invites his readers to suppose that his friend has announced his New Year's resolution to him—"that he will give up eating meat on" January 1 (1999, p. 254). He reports that if he finds his friend eating meat on New Year's Eve, he "cannot scorn him for his weakness of will" even though he can scorn him for weakness of will if he finds him eating meat the next day. Holton adds: "His views about what is best have not changed over the two days; the difference stems from the intention."

Consider the following case. My friend Matt tells me that some philosophical arguments convinced him today that, in Holton's words, "he should not eat meat" (1999, p. 252). He also tells me that he has spent a lot of money on fancy steaks and ribs for a New Year's Eve party he is hosting tonight and that he will be absolutely miserable at the party and decrease the probability that his friends will have a good time if he does not participate in the meat eating. In light of various considerations, including the philosophical arguments and his beliefs about his own state of mind, Matt judges it best on the whole to give up eating meat tomorrow morning—not today. His eating meat today does not count as a core akratic action (see section 1); but, other things being equal, his eating meat tomorrow would so count. Depending on how Matt's belief that "he should not eat meat" is to be understood, it might not change over the two days. But on New Year's Eve he believes it best to quit tomorrow, and on New Year's morning he believes it best to quit right then. That is a significant difference.

I presented Matt's case to highlight a problem with Holton's story about his meat-eating friend. We can see how someone who believes that "he should not eat meat" might not believe that it would be best (on the whole) not to eat meat today. If although Holton's friend has the former belief, he eats meat at a time at which he lacks the belief that it would be best to refrain from eating meat then, his meat eating is not a core akratic action. But if, instead, he *has* the latter belief at the time, why should we judge that his uncompelled meat eating, although it is akratic, displays no weakness of will? Why should we not believe that, in the absence of any weakness of will, Holton's friend would act as he judged best? If we were already convinced that "our ordinary notion of weakness of will" (Holton 1999, p. 262) is such that unless "cases of *akrasia* . . . involve an unreasonable revision of intention, they are not cases of weakness of will" (p. 255), we would know where to look for our answer. But Holton's story about the meat eater is offered as support for this thesis about our ordinary notion of weakness of will. It is supposed to help move his readers toward acceptance of his thesis about that notion.

How easy one thinks it is to generate vignettes in which agents who perform a core akratic action display no weakness of will depends, in part, on how one conceives of the judgment that the agents are supposed to act against. If one conceives of this judgment as, for example, something that can express the upshot of a purely academic exercise that has no interesting connection to the agent's motivational condition, one may find it easy to imagine what seem to be core akratic actions that do not involve weakness of will. Given a very undemanding conception of the judgment at issue, one might imagine cases in which someone who seemingly judges it best on the whole to A has no inclination at all to A and freely does something else instead. When an agent feels no pull at all toward the course of action he judges best, the claim that he displays weakness of will seems out of place. If instead one conceives of the A-favoring better judgment at issue as something that can only be produced by practical reasoning and as tightly connected—conceptually or causally—to motivation to A or to intending to A, one will tend to regard vignettes of the imagined kind as falling short of being stories about core akratic action owing to the absence of a judgment of the required sort. A review of the literature on akrasia would show that those who reject akratic action as conceptually or psychologically impossible conceive of the judgment at issue as very tightly connected to intention, motivation, or both (see Mele 1987, chs. 1 and 2). Those who regard core akratic action as theoretically challenging but psychologically possible view this connection as relatively tight but defeasible (for reviews, see Stroud 2008 and Walker 1989; also see Davidson 1970 and Mele 1987, chs. 3 and 6). The weaker the connection one postulates here, the more plausible it will seem that in performing some core akratic actions agents display no weakness of will. But one who conceives of better judgment in such a way that it is only weakly connected to motivation and intention runs the risk of changing the subject.

I turn to a related issue. Recall Holton's claim that "To display weakness of will, an agent must have formed [a resolution] that he revises" (1999, p. 259). This is a bold claim. Holton realizes that some readers will be inclined to suggest that weakness of will is at least sometimes displayed in cases in which "a person fails to form an intention to do what he knows to be best, and as a result does what he knows not to be" (p. 257). Indeed, Donald Davidson's enormously influential article "How Is Weakness of the Will Possible?" (1970) defends, in effect, the proposition that in all cases of weakness of will the agent irrationally fails to move from an all-things-considered better judgment to a corresponding intention. (For an explanation of the expression "in effect" in the preceding sentence, see Mele 1987, pp. 33–34. On cases of weakness of will that involve the agent's not intending to A even though he judges it best to A, also see Audi 1979 and Davidson 1985b, pp. 205–6.) Holton reports that if it is true that agents sometimes display weakness of will in scenarios of the kind at issue, he "should rest content with the claim that many cases of weakness of will are captured" by his account (1999, p. 258). But he is disinclined to settle for the more modest proposal: "I cannot help thinking that the traditional account is not simply inadequate, but straight-out wrong."

Holton asserts that "if we are to get a really compelling counterexample" to his claim that displaying weakness of will requires revising a resolution, "we need a clear case of weakness of will in which a person knows that, if he were to form the intention to do what he judges best, he would stick to that intention; but he fails to form the intention" (1999, p. 258). He adds that he is "unable to think of one." I do not see why we have to go this far—particularly, why this *knowledge* is required—to get a successful counterexample, but I set that fact about me aside for now.

Consider the following case from *Irrationality*:

> Mike, who is visiting New Orleans for the first time, is strolling down Bourbon Street when he notices a number of clubs featuring strip-tease acts. He has never before seen ecdysiasts perform, and he would like to take this opportunity to do so. However, he has moral qualms. He believes that watching ecdysiasts, though by no means seriously wrong, is somewhat exploitive of women. Though Mike does not believe that moral reasons are always the better reasons for action, he does judge that he has slightly better reason, all things considered, not to enter the clubs than to enter them. Now, Mike has a painless desire-eradicating device in his pocket. He realizes that he can bring it about that he acts on his better judgment simply by pressing a button: in the absence of a desire to see ecdysiasts he certainly would not enter a strip joint. But he decides to indulge himself—against his better judgment. (Mele 1987, p. 28)

We can suppose that Mike knows that if he were to resolve not to enter the building, he would press the button and refrain from entering.

Does Mike display no weakness of will at all in this story? As in the case of Christabel's imagined akratic action of embarking on the affair, some readers may be inclined to believe that, in the absence of any weakness of will, Mike would have resolved not to enter the building and would have acted accordingly. A person with a stronger will, they might think, would not have succumbed to temptation. Holton may claim that such readers are confusing "our ordinary notion of weakness of will" (1999, p. 262) with akrasia. But, as I have explained, the studies I reported indicate that this ordinary notion is much closer to a relatively standard conception of akrasia than Holton would have us believe.

I turn to another case (see Mele 2000a, p. 84). This time there is no magical device, but there also is no supposition that the agent "knows that, if he were to form the intention to do what he judges best, he would stick to that intention" (Holton 1999, p. 258). Joe has believed for quite some time that it would be best to quit smoking cigarettes, and he is thinking yet again—this time on New Year's Eve—about when to quit. He is confident both that quitting will be extremely hard and that, unless he is careful to pick a good time to embark on that project, he will fail. Joe knows that the first week of January tends not to be a busy time for him at work, and he believes that the thought of making a fresh start on life at the beginning of a new year may be useful to him. After further reflection, he judges that it would be best to smoke his last cigarette tonight and to be smoke free from then on. When Joe reports this to Jill, his partner, she asks whether this is his New Year's resolution. He sincerely replies, "Not yet. I haven't yet decided to quit tomorrow. Making that decision will be hard. To make it, I'll really have to psych myself up. I've been smoking for forty years. I believe that I can quit, but I would definitely miss smoking."

I wish this story had a happy ending; but as it happens, Joe fails to decide to quit smoking, despite his better judgment. Tomorrow, he smokes less than usual, but he has his first cigarette minutes after he awakes, as always. By hypothesis, he could have decided to quit, and if he had so decided, he would have been smoke free from New Year's day on.

Joe does not revise any resolutions in this story. Even so, he certainly seems to display some weakness of will. At least it certainly seems that way to me. Readers are free to make their own judgments about Joe, of course. Any readers who are confident that, although Joe acts akratically, he displays no weakness of will because they are convinced that the ordinary notion of weakness of will—unlike the notion of akrasia—features resolution revision and does not feature acting contrary to one's better judgment should review the results of the two studies I discussed. They should also attend to the results of the studies to be described shortly.

Perhaps the clearest cases of weakness of will are those in which agents both judge it best to *A* and intend to *A*.[9] Those are the cases that receive the most attention in *Irrationality*, because they are the cases of weakness of will (and instances of akratic action) that seem to call out the loudest for explanation. Holton and I agree that, in these cases, agents display some weakness of will (provided that the intention is what Holton calls a resolution). We also agree that there are cases of weakness of will in which agents do not act contrary to a better judgment. We disagree about cases like Joe's.

The third study I conducted featured a simplified version of Joe's story (see note 10).[10] Participants were twenty-five undergraduates at Florida State University. They were in the eleventh week of their first philosophy course—an elementary logic course—and weakness of will was not on their course agenda. Students were informed of the experimenter's interest in how they understood the expression "weakness of will." They were given a seven-point scale—with 1 labeled "strongly agree" and 7 labeled "strongly disagree"—and asked to mark their response to the following assertion by circling a number: "Joe displays some weakness of will in this story."

The mean response was 2.68, and twenty of the twenty-five students (80%) agreed with the assertion (that is, gave responses of 1, 2, or 3) whereas only four (16%) disagreed with it (that is, gave answers of 5, 6, or 7). Obviously, this is evidence that an ordinary notion of weakness of will is such that Joe counts as displaying weakness of will—even though he does not act contrary to an intention. What he does act contrary to is his better judgment.[11]

My fourth study provides additional evidence for this proposition about an ordinary notion of weakness of will. In study 4, I used the same simplified version of Joe's story as in study 3 and I presented the same information about the experimenter's interest. Participants were one hundred undergraduates at Florida State University. They were in the second week of their first philosophy course, and weakness of will was not on the course agenda. The students were presented with the following question and asked to answer it by circling "Yes" or "No": "Does Joe display any weakness of will in this story?" The results were unsurprising, given the results of study 3: seventy-three said yes and twenty-seven said no. Here again, even though Joe does not act contrary to an intention, a strong majority (73%) say that he displays weakness of will.

Might many of the respondents who say that Joe displays some weakness of will in this story be thinking that he displays it, not in failing to quit smoking, but in some other way (see May and Holton n.d.)? And might I be making it too easy for participants to answer yes by asking whether Joe displays *any* (or *some*) weakness of will (see May and Holton n.d.)? Both questions are reasonable. To get evidence about these issues, I conducted a fifth study. I used the same story as in studies 3 and 4 and the same statement of interest, but this time I asked participants to mark their responses to the following assertion: "Joe displays weakness of will in failing to quit smoking." The options were "yes" and "no."

Participants were sixty-four undergraduates at Florida State University. They were in the first week of a basic philosophy course, and, again, weakness of will was not on their syllabus. About 80% answered yes and about 20% answered no (79.6875% versus 20.3125%). The change did not weaken the response.

Holton describes a case in which an agent who judges it best to A does not resolve to A "because he knows that he would not be able to go through with it" (1999, p. 258).

He writes: "It is because he knows that he is someone with a tendency to weakness of will that he acts as he does. So, on the account given here, his weakness of will explains his action.... It seems to me that is good enough. Once we have said that we feel no need to insist that [he] actually exhibits weakness of will here." Part of Holton's aim here may be to offer a diagnosis of why someone might mistakenly believe that the agent exhibits weakness of will: the alleged mistake derives perhaps from regarding the fact that weakness of will explains someone's action as sufficient for its being true that the agent *exhibits* weakness of will. Be this as it may, this error theory does not apply to Joe's story. Joe reports that he believes that he can quit (both in the story spun above and in the simplified version used in studies 3, 4, and 5). It is no part of Joe's story that "he knows that he would not be able to go through with [quitting smoking]" (p. 258).

3. Weakness of Will and Compulsion

One necessary condition for an action's being akratic, on a standard conception, is that it is uncompelled. A heroin addict who judges it best not to use the drug now but uses it now because he has an irresistible desire to do so does not count as akratically using the drug. A thrill seeker who, in the absence of compulsion and against his better judgment, uses the drug for the first time may use it akratically (see Mele 1987, p. 4). Holton reports that "it is not obvious" to him that "it would be a disaster" if his account of weakness of will "did classify compulsive acts as weak willed; for it is not obvious to me that they are not" (1999, p. 261).

I would not be surprised if many—and even most—lay respondents to a story in which it is made clear that an agent is moved by an irresistible desire would, if asked, say that he displays some weakness of will. Some respondents who give this response may think that if the agent's will were not weak, he would be able to resist the desire and that the desire's being irresistible by him entails some weakness of will. But if this is how they are thinking, they should be expected to say that an agent who acts on an irresistible desire displays some weakness of will even if he does not revise any resolutions (and even if what he does is not contrary to a better judgment). If an "ordinary notion of weakness of will" (Holton 1999, p. 262) were to be such that a heroin addict who revises his resolution not to use the drug today and uses it owing to an irresistible desire for the drug is properly said to display weakness of will, it might also be such that this addict would properly be said to display weakness of will even if he revised no resolution (and acted contrary to no better judgment). Such a notion of weakness of will is remote from a traditional notion of akrasia; it also is a philosophically less interesting notion.

The occurrence of core akratic actions seems to be an unfortunate fact of life. Unlike many such (apparent) facts, this one has attracted considerable philosophical attention for nearly two and a half millennia. A major source of the interest is not far to seek: core akratic action, if it is a genuine phenomenon, raises difficult questions about the connection between our evaluative judgments about prospective courses of action and our intentional actions, an important connection for any theory of the explanation of intentional behavior that accords our evaluative judgments a role in explaining some of our intentional actions. How are considered judgments about what it is best to do connected to actions if it is possible consciously to believe that it is best, on the whole, to A now and yet freely do something else instead? That is an interesting and challenging question—one on which an enormous amount of time and effort has been spent over a great many years. If an equally interesting challenge is raised by a notion of weakness of will that counts some agents who act on irresistible desires as displaying that property, I do not know what it is.

Holton contends that if no compulsive acts are weak willed, "a simple amendment to the account would fix things up. Rather than say that weakness of will consists in over-readily revising [a resolution], say that it consists in over-readily revising [a resolution] *when it is in the agent's power to desist from that revision*" (1999 p. 262). He is not committed to a more inclusive notion of weakness of will than the one captured by the amended account.[12] In a subsequent article, he reports that on his account of weakness of will, "the interesting question would no longer be how *weakness* of will is possible. It is all too easy to see how an earlier resolution could be overcome by the growth of a subsequent desire" (2003, p. 39). (The interesting question, he says, "would be how *strength* of will is possible.")

A correct account of "our ordinary notion of weakness of will" (Holton 1999, p. 262) might be useful for some purposes even if no particularly interesting philosophical issues are raised by the notion. However, as I have shown, there is good reason to deny that Holton has provided such an account. The survey studies conducted so far indicate that my own view of the nature of akratic action (sketched in section 1) is more congruent with our ordinary notion of weakness of will than Holton's account is.[13] Ancient work on akratic action was focused on a theoretically challenging question, and applications of modern methods suggest that the question can be formulated adequately in terms of an ordinary present-day notion of weakness of will.

THREE

• • •

Weakness and Compulsion

Some philosophers worry about whether weak-willed actions are distinguishable from actions that agents are *compelled* to perform.¹ I define *core weak-willed* action as free (and therefore uncompelled), sane, intentional action that, as the nondepressed agent consciously recognizes at the time of action, is contrary to his better judgment, a judgment based on practical reasoning.² (As shorthand for this, I use "free action contrary to the agent's *J*." A central question of this chapter can then be expressed in shorthand as follows: Has it been shown that, even if some actions are free, no actions contrary to an agent's *J* can be free?) Seemingly, today, as in Socrates's time (Plato, *Protagoras* 352b–358d), many people believe that there are core weak-willed actions. And many philosophers maintain that core weak-willed action is a genuine phenomenon. The worry that is the topic of this chapter is that until it has been explained how alleged core weak-willed actions differ from compelled (hence unfree) actions contrary to the agent's better judgment, people have no right to believe that core weak-willed actions occur.

One might hope to find a way of laying this worry to rest without uncovering the truth about free will. However, our prospects of satisfying that hope look dim. If compatibilists (proponents of the thesis that free will is compatible with determinism) are mistaken in holding that there is a difference between compulsion (that is, being compelled to do something) and deterministic causation, then the occurrence of core weak-willed actions depends on the truth of libertarianism (the conjunction of incompatibilism and the thesis that there are free actions).[3] If free or uncompelled action requires that one could have acted otherwise, and traditional compatibilists are wrong in thinking that, in a suitable sense, one could have acted otherwise in a deterministic world, then, again, any adequate account of core weak-willed action must be libertarian. If, however, libertarians face insoluble problems about luck and control, no libertarian account of weak-willed action can work.[4] And if it is a mystery how indeterminism can contribute to free action (Fischer 1994, ch. 7, especially p. 141; van Inwagen 2000), libertarian accounts of weak-willed action are bound to be mysterious. Things look really tough. It may seem that not another word should be written about weakness of will (or at least core weak-willed action) until we have solved the free will problem(s).

Despite appearances, one can make progress on the topic without defending an account of free will. In section 1, I criticize a pair of arguments for the nonexistence of core weak-willed action with a view to setting the stage for a more general discussion of the lay of the land. In sections 2 and 3, I argue that the worry to which this chapter is addressed is seriously inflated.

1. Two Unsuccessful Arguments for Skepticism about Core Weak-Willed Action

Philosophers who contend that there are no core weak-willed actions (for example, Hare 1963, ch. 5; Pugmire 1982; Watson 1977) do not base their arguments for that thesis on arguments for the thesis that there are no free actions. An argument so based would be as uninteresting as an argument so grounded for the thesis that people never freely eat tofu. If one shows that there are no free actions at all, one can leave it to one's readers to infer that there are no free actions of specific kinds, including tofu consumption and core weak-willed actions. For the purposes of this chapter, it can be assumed that at least some actions are free. It can then be asked whether there are good grounds for believing that although some actions are free, no alleged core weak-willed actions—or no actions contrary to an agent's *J*—are among them.

A related assumption also is in order. Theorists who deny that there are core weak-willed actions can hold (1) that no intentional actions are contrary to the agent's *J*, or (2) that all intentional actions that are contrary to the agent's *J* are unfree. The first line is a hard one to take. It is plausible that some compulsive hand-washers, compulsive liars, or crack cocaine addicts, for example, are occasionally compelled to perform intentional actions that they judge it best not to perform on the basis of practical reasoning and consciously recognize at the time to be contrary to their better judgment.[5] Of course, theoretical maneuvers are possible. It can be claimed, for example, that the nature of human agency is such that a human *agent* acts only if the action is guided by (or not at odds with) the human being's better judgment—that when this is not so, something less, or other, than the agent is acting. Elsewhere, I have defended the view that human agents are simply human beings who act (Mele 2003, ch. 10), and I judge it best not to repeat the arguments here. In any case, if there are no unfree intentional actions contrary to the agent's better judgment, the worry that is the topic of this chapter is groundless. A more concise statement of that worry is that until it has been explained how alleged core weak-willed actions differ from unfree actions contrary to the agent's *J*, people have no right to believe that human agents ever perform core weak-willed actions. Therefore, for the purposes of this chapter, it is assumed not only that some intentional actions are free but also that some intentional actions are contrary to the agent's *J*.

These assumptions are labeled for ease of reference:

P1. Some intentional actions are free.
P2. Some intentional actions are contrary to the agent's J.

P1, P2, and the following assertion form a consistent trio:

UF. All intentional actions contrary to the agent's J are unfree.

How might a philosopher try to defend UF while granting P1 and P2? Here is a sketch of one such defense.

Argument A
A1. Holding at t a judgment that it is best to A at t is conceptually sufficient for intending at t to A at t.
A2. Any agent who intends at a time to A then but does not A then is unable to A at the time.
A3. Such an agent, being unable to A, is compelled to perform—and therefore unfreely performs—whatever pertinent intentional action he performs at the time.[6]

Premise A2 is falsified by simple counterexamples. A good pitcher might intend to throw a pitch in the strike zone and accidentally miss, even though he was able to do what he intended. It may be replied that the failures in alleged cases of core weak-willed action are of a different kind and that A2 simply needs to be revised to capture the difference. Perhaps it will be suggested that in alleged cases of core weak-willed action, the failure involves a change of intention—for example, a change from intending to order a diet coke to intending to order a regular coke—whereas the pitcher's failure does not. Now, either the change of intention is paired with a corresponding change of judgment or it is not. If it is, then the action that executes the new intention is not a core weak-willed action, for it is not contrary to the agent's better judgment *at the time of action*. A constituent of this point is more important for immediate purposes: if there is a change of judgment that matches the change of intention, then the agent does not act contrary to his J in executing that intention. Given P2, some actions *are* contrary to the agent's

J, and what the skeptic is supposed to be doing now is producing an argument that all such actions are unfree. The skeptic cannot do that without making claims about agents who act contrary to their *J*, and the skeptic who is advancing argument *A* cannot perform that trick without making claims about agents' abilities in such cases. If, on the other hand, the change of intention is *not* paired with a corresponding change of judgment, then *A1* is threatened. Premise *A1*, again, is the assertion that holding at *t* a judgment that it is best to *A* at *t* is conceptually sufficient for intending at *t* to *A* at *t*. This assertion is falsified by an agent who had intended in accordance with such a judgment but no longer so intends, even though the judgment persists. The problem of suitably modifying *A2* is left as an exercise for the skeptic.

Now for a problem with *A1*. Given *P2*, *A1* is in dire straits. Consider a compulsive hand-washer, a compulsive liar, or a crack cocaine addict who believes on the basis of practical reasoning that it is best not to wash his hands now, not to tell a certain lie now, or not to use crack now, but who does it anyway, intentionally and unfreely. If *A1* is true, this agent is intentionally washing his hands, telling a certain lie, or using crack while intending not to do so. Although this may be conceptually possible—for example, perhaps a commissurotomized agent may intend not to *A* while also intending to *A* and acting on the latter intention (also see chapter 4, note 2, on anarchic hand syndrome)—it is a highly implausible hypothesis about representative cases of the kind at issue. A much more plausible hypothesis is that although the troubled agent believes that it would be best not to wash his hands now, not to tell that lie now, or not to use crack now, he lacks a corresponding intention and instead intends to do what he is doing.

Proposition *A3* also is problematic. Imagine an agent who has been dieting and who judges it best to order a low-calorie cottage cheese salad for lunch today. Unfortunately, he is sorely tempted by several other items on the menu, including a hamburger, a philly cheese steak, and a roast pork sandwich. He orders the cheese steak. Even if the agent was unable to order the salad, we would need an argument that he was compelled to order the cheese steak—that, for example, ordering the burger was not open to him. Then again, perhaps it will be claimed that the compelled action is ordering something other than the salad, or not ordering the salad.[7] Skeptics about weak-willed action are encouraged to develop a reading of *A3* suitable for their purposes. Perhaps they will consider claiming (1) that even if not all intentional actions contrary to the agent's *J* are compelled, all intentional actions contrary to the agent's *J* at least resemble compelled actions contrary to an agent's *J* in that the agent was unable to act in accordance with his *J*, and (2) that being unable to act in accordance with one's *J* is sufficient for the unfreedom of the contrary action performed. This thought receives attention in section 2.

Gary Watson offers the following argument for *UF* (1977, pp. 336–38):

Argument B

B1. An agent's succumbing to a desire contrary to his better judgment cannot be explained by his choosing not to resist, nor by his making a culpably insufficient effort to resist.

B2. Only one explanation remains: the agent was *unable* to resist.

So *UF.* All intentional actions contrary to the agent's better judgment are unfree.

An agent's choosing not to resist, Watson argues, cannot explain core weak-willed action, for to make such a choice "would be to change" one's better judgment (p. 337). For example, "The weak drinker's failure to resist her desire to drink is a failure to implement her choice not to drink. To choose not to implement this choice would be to change her original judgment, and the case would no longer be a case of failure to implement a judgment" (pp. 336–37). Watson also contends that an insufficient effort cannot be due to a judgment that the effort is not worth the trouble, because the judgment that it *is* worth the trouble is implicit in the violated better judgment (p. 338). Nor, he argues, can the insufficient effort be explained by a misjudgment of "the amount of effort required," for misjudgment is "a different fault from weakness of will" (p. 338).

Start with the weak drinker. Assuming that this agent chooses not to drink but drinks anyway, it is true that in succumbing to her desire for a drink she fails "to implement her choice not to drink." But it is difficult to see why one should say, with Watson, that the agent "chooses not to implement her choice" not to drink. Why not say that instead of making that second-order choice, the agent chooses to drink and abandons her choice not to drink? The context suggests that Watson identifies an agent's choosing not to implement a choice that matches her better judgment with her choosing not to resist the pertinent desire. In any case, whether the agent makes the second-order choice Watson mentions, the first-order choice to drink, the choice not to resist her desire to drink, or any number of these choices, we are faced with the question whether to make that choice "would be to change her original judgment."

In some alleged cases of core weak-willed action, agents judge it best to *A* straightaway, choose, decide, or intend accordingly, and backslide, while retaining their judgment (see Mele 1987, ch. 3). In others, agents who judge it best to *A* straightaway do not choose, decide, or intend accordingly (see Audi 1979, p. 191; Davidson 1980, ch. 2; Mele 1992a, pp. 228–34; Rorty 1980b). In the passage I quoted about the weak drinker, Watson evidently has the former kind of case in mind. It will be useful to attend first to a case of the latter kind. Imagine, if you can, that Drew, who has had one shot of whiskey and needs to drive home soon, judges it best to switch now to coffee but neither chooses, decides, nor intends accordingly. She intentionally takes another whiskey. The reader is not asked to imagine that Drew displays weakness of will in drinking the second shot of whiskey; it is left open that she drinks it unfreely. I have already argued that given *P2*, which Watson accepts, it is very plausible that some agents who judge at *t* that it is best to *A* at *t* do not have a corresponding intention at *t* and intend a course of action that is at odds with that judgment. A crack addict might judge (believe) it best not to use crack now, lack an intention not to use it now, intend to use it now, and intentionally use it now. If this is true, we would need a special reason for claiming that whenever an agent makes a judgment that it is best to *A*, he chooses to *A*. If an agent's *holding* a judgment (believing) that it is best to *A* need not be paired with his having a corresponding intention, why should we think that an agent's *making* a judgment that it is best to *A* must be paired with his making a corresponding choice or forming a corresponding intention? Watson does not answer this question.

In any case, *if* Drew can judge it best not to drink a second whiskey without choosing accordingly, then she can fail "to resist her desire to drink" without there being any failure on her part "to implement her choice not to drink." If she makes no such choice, she does not fail to implement it. And if there is no such failure of implementation, then the reason Watson offers for maintaining that the agent "change[d] her original judgment" is undercut.

A scenario in which a judgment-matching choice is made will be discussed shortly. The plausibility of scenarios of the present sort deserves a bit more attention now. Recall the stories about Joe the smoker and Mike the tourist in chapter 2 (section 2). These stories at least have the appearance of coherence. Seemingly, although Joe decides that it would be best to quit smoking, he may or may not form the intention (choose, decide) to quit. Similarly, it seems that Mike's better judgment about entering the strip-tease bar may or may not be matched by a corresponding choice or decision. In any case, there is no argument for the incoherence of stories of this kind in Watson's essay. (I am not claiming now that either agent acts freely.)[8]

If Drew can fail to resist her desire for a second whiskey without changing her judgment about what it is best to do, what about Donna, who, like Drew, takes another whiskey despite judging it best to switch now from whiskey to coffee, but, unlike Drew, chooses to switch now to coffee when she makes her judgment? Watson would say (*W1*) that Donna's "failure to resist her desire to drink [a second whiskey] is a failure to implement her choice not to drink," (*W2a*) that "to choose not to implement this choice [is] to change her original judgment," (*W2b*) that to choose not to resist her desire to drink a second whiskey is to change that judgment, and (*W3*) that Donna's drinking the second whiskey therefore is not a core weak-willed action, since it is not contrary to her better judgment (1977, pp. 336–37). Is *W2a* or *W2b* true? There is no argument for either in Watson's essay, and some stories in which analogues of both are false certainly seem coherent.

Here is one such story (see Mele 1987, p. 25). Alex's friend, Bob, has proposed that they affirm their friendship by becoming blood brothers, because Alex is about to go away to prep school. The ceremony involves the boys' cutting their own right palms with a pocket knife and then shaking hands so that their blood will mingle. Alex is averse to cutting himself, but he carefully weighs his reasons for accepting the proposal against his competing reasons (including his aversion) and he judges that it would be best to accept the proposal and to perform the ceremony at once. He chooses, accordingly, to cut his hand with the knife straightaway, thus forming an intention to do so. Without considering that he may find the task difficult, he grasps the knife and moves it toward his right palm with the intention of drawing blood. However, as he sees the knife come very close to his skin, he intentionally stops, owing significantly to his aversion. He chooses not to implement his original choice just now, and he chooses not to resist his aversion further just now. Alex abandons his original choice. But he has not changed his mind about what it is best to do, and he is upset with himself for chickening out. (Soon, Alex resolves to try again, this time without looking. The second attempt succeeds.)

If this story is incoherent, Watson needs to explain why. If he were to assent to *A1*—the thesis that holding at t a judgment that it is best to A at t is conceptually sufficient for intending at t to A at t—he could appeal to it here: because Alex no longer intends to cut his hand straightaway, it would follow that he no longer judges that it would be best to cut it straightaway. But Watson rejects *A1* to accommodate compulsives who act contrary to their better judgment.

The topic under discussion has been Watson's argument for an element of the first premise of argument *B*. The element is this: (*B1a*) An agent's succumbing to a desire contrary to his better judgment cannot be explained by his choosing not to resist.[9] One may try an alternative line of defense, arguing that it is illegitimate to explain an alleged weak-willed action by appealing to a choice not to resist, because such a choice, if free, would itself be a weak-willed action (see Tenenbaum 1999, pp. 888–89). The thought is that one cannot explain how a weak-willed action happens by appealing to a weak-willed action in the explanans. However, this argument cannot support argument *B*. The procedural claim that one cannot explain, *for the reason just cited*, a weak-willed succumbing to a desire by appealing to a weak-willed choice not to resist does nothing to support the premise (*B2*) that the only explanation that remains is that the agent was unable to resist; and, of course, the function of *B1* in argument *B* is to support this premise. The procedural claim is compatible with its being the case (1) that something, x, accounts for the agent's weak-willed choice not to resist, and thereby plays a significant role in accounting for the alleged weak-willed action at issue; (2) that x and the entire explanatory story are consistent with the agent's being able to resist temptation; and (3) that x is not itself a weak-willed (overt or mental) action. Various views about what x might be are present in the literature (see Mele 1987, pp. 93–95). I return to this matter in subsequent chapters.

2. Three Skeptical Theses

It may seem that the next order of business should be to argue for the possibility of core weak-willed actions, benefiting from the criticisms offered here of arguments *A* and *B*. In *Irrationality* (1987), I offer arguments for the possibility of core weak-willed actions and a detailed account of the etiology of such actions, but I take compatibilism for granted there. Treating libertarianism (hence incompatibilism) as a live option complicates matters considerably. Again, one defining characteristic of core weak-willed actions is that they are free. For the purposes of this chapter, as I have explained, it is legitimate to assume that there are free actions. However, one cannot persuade a deeply skeptical audience that free actions contrary to one's *J* are possible without first showing what free action is—or, if both compatibilism and libertarianism are left open, without developing attractive compatibilist and libertarian accounts of free action. These freedom-focused projects are beyond the scope of this book. (In Mele 2006a, I develop two detailed accounts of free action—one for compatibilists and the other for libertarians). It can reasonably be claimed that in the absence of a convincing argument for UF, there is a presumption in favor of the common-sense view that there are core weak-willed actions. But one should hope to get further than that.

Why do ordinary folks believe that there are (in my terminology, not theirs) core weak-willed actions? Presumably, largely because they take themselves to have firsthand experience of such actions and partly because some of their observations of—and conversations with—others indicate to them that they are not alone in this. It seems to them that, occasionally, they perform, in the absence of compulsion, intentional actions that are contrary to their *J*. They have, at such times, no feeling of being compelled. Indeed, they may feel free and uncompelled, and they may believe at the time of action that they are able to do what they judge best at the time.

It is possible that these ordinary agents are wrong about this, of course. After all, it is possible that malicious Martians compel them to do everything they do—or selectively compel them to do what they do in cases in which they think they are acting in a weak-willed way—and cause them to have the aforementioned feelings and beliefs about themselves. But why should one believe that they are wrong? And, more germane for the purposes of this chapter, why should one believe that they are wrong even while one believes that some actions are free? Arguments *A* and *B* purport to answer these questions. But I have shown that these arguments are unpersuasive.

The assumption, *P1*, that some intentional actions are free is in place. Philosophers who propose to defend the thesis, *UF*, that all intentional actions contrary to the agent's *J* are unfree (in which case there are no core weak-willed actions) while granting *P1* have some strategic options. They can defend any of the following theses.

1. *The no-matter-what thesis*: *UF* is true no matter which of the various actual or possible pro free action views is correct (for example, a traditional compatibilist view or an agent-causal libertarian view).[10]
2. *The know-it-all thesis*: The correct pro free action view entails *UF*, even if some actions contrary to the agent's *J* would be free if some of the alternative views were correct.
3. *The know-what-matters thesis*: Some true thesis about free action entails *UF*, even if some actions contrary to the agent's *J* would be free if some of the pro free action views that do not endorse that thesis were correct.

The two arguments for *UF* criticized in section 1—arguments *A* and *B*—could be read as arguments for the no-matter-what thesis if it were not an option to reject the ability constraints on free action to which they appeal. Semicompatibilists hold that determinism is compatible with moral responsibility and free action even if it is incompatible with agents' ever having been able to act otherwise than they did (Fischer 1994, 2006; Fischer and Ravizza 1998). They contend that acting freely does not require an ability of this kind; but the proponent of argument *A* seeks to demonstrate the unfreedom of actions contrary to the agent's *J* partly on the basis of the claim that the agent was unable to take the course of action that he judged best, and the proponent of argument *B* appeals, for the same purpose, to the agent's alleged inability successfully to resist the desire on which he acted. Semicompatibilism's leading advocates explicitly make room for weak-willed actions in their accounts of the kind of reasons-responsiveness that is crucial for moral responsibility and free action (Fischer 1994, pp. 164–68; Fischer and Ravizza 1998, pp. 41–45, 68). According to them, it is possible that an agent who *A*-ed contrary to his *J* freely *A*-ed and was morally responsible for *A*-ing, even if he was unable to act in accordance with his *J* and unable successfully to resist his desire to *A*.

A proponent of *UF* may argue that on any pro free action view with a *correct* ability constraint, unlike semicompatibilism, *UF* is true. This would be a defense of the know-what-matters thesis. Such a philosopher needs to produce a convincing argument that semicompatibilism is false.

Semicompatibilism is motivated partly by Frankfurt-style cases (see Frankfurt 1969), a style of thought-experiment to be discussed shortly. An observation about compulsion and the ability to act otherwise is in order in this connection. Consideration of a representative case of apparent core weak-willed action and a Frankfurt-style variant of that case will prepare the way for it. Return to Drew and consider things from her point of view. Because she has had one shot of whiskey already—and very recently—at the party she is attending and needs to drive home soon, she judges it best to switch now to coffee. She believes both that she can switch from whiskey to coffee now and that she can have another whiskey now instead; in Drew's opinion, it is up to her which of these she does. She knows that it is risky to drive under the influence of two shots and she judges that, in light of the risk, her reason for having a second shot—that she would enjoy it—does not justify having one. Although Drew judges that she should switch to coffee, she thinks "I've had a bit too much to drink before and all has gone well. I really should switch to coffee, but I'll indulge myself. Just one more shot, then a cup of coffee, then I'll drive home." Still believing that it would be best to switch to coffee now, Drew decides to drink another shot and drinks one. She does not feel compelled to drink. She feels that she is deciding freely and that she is freely drinking the whiskey.

The next case on the agenda is a Frankfurt-style variant. Frankfurt-style cases are controversial, but many philosophers have been persuaded by them that an agent who could not have done otherwise than A may nevertheless be morally responsible for A-ing and A freely, and Mele and Robb (1998) features what is argued to be a coherent, successful case of this kind (also see Mele and Robb 2003).[11] I do not discuss the controversy here. Instead, I sketch a simple Frankfurt-style variant of Drew's case and discuss an implication that holds *if* the case is successful.

Imagine Drew's story with an extra feature. A neurosurgeon has tinkered with Drew's brain in such a way that if she had not, at t, decided on her own to have a second whiskey then, a certain brain process, B, would have resulted, at t, in her deciding to drink another whiskey then. B did not in any way interfere with Drew's reasoning, her decision-making, or her experiences, and the only thing that could have preempted B, given that Drew was capable of making a decision at t, was her deciding on her own then to have a second whiskey then. Libertarians can imagine that Drew made her decision in a way they think free decisions are made—for example, that she agent-caused it in a normal way or that it issued in a normal event-causal way from an appropriate kind of indeterministic process. They can imagine that Drew's world is indeterministic in a way that promotes free action. Compatibilists can also imagine that Drew made her decision in a suitable way. And compatibilists who hold that free action requires the truth of determinism can imagine a deterministic version of the story in which Drew decides in a suitable way.[12] Now, Drew's decision was to have a second whiskey *then*. So there was not much time for her to change her decision after making it. But *B* also was such that if Drew were to waver, it would prevent her from changing her decision. Since Drew did not waver, *B* was idle in this connection too.

If the original case is a case of uncompelled, free decision and overt action, and *if* this Frankfurt-style case is coherent, then, plausibly, Drew's pertinent decision and action are uncompelled and free in the latter case too—even though she could not have done otherwise than decide on the second whiskey and drink it. After all, *B* was idle with respect to Drew's decision to drink and her drinking. Arguments that no Frankfurt-style case of the sort sketched is successful may be forthcoming. (For a reply to several extant arguments for this thesis, see Mele and Robb 2003.) When they are produced, they can be assessed. But until it is shown that no Frankfurt-style case can hit its mark, it is very risky to take it for granted that an agent who could not have acted in accordance with her *J* unfreely acted as she did. Philosophers who hold that what seem to be core weak-willed actions are really compelled actions should produce an account of an action *A*'s being compelled that does not assume that the fact that the agent could not have done otherwise than *A* is sufficient for such compulsion, and they should produce arguments for *UF* that do not assume that the fact that an agent who *A*-ed contrary to his *J* could not have acted in accordance with his *J* is sufficient for his having *A*-ed unfreely. Proponents of *UF* have their work cut out for them.

The know-it-all thesis is next on the agenda. Pro free action views divide into libertarian and compatibilist views. There are many versions of each. It would be surprising if garden-variety libertarians were to endorse *UF*. Stock libertarian examples of free choices and other free actions feature agents in internal conflict, including conflicts between better judgments and desires. The standard claim is that a choice made in the right way and an action executing that choice are free whether the choice and subsequent action accord with the agent's *J* or are contrary to it (Kane 1996, pp. 126–33; van Inwagen 2000).

Semicompatibilism is a version of compatibilism. Traditional versions of compatibilism include the theses that free action requires the ability to act otherwise than one does and that this ability is compatible with determinism. Traditional compatibilists rely on a distinction between compulsion and causation (see note 3) and argue that although an action's being compelled precludes its being a free action, an action's being deterministically caused does not. One relevant question, for present purposes, is whether any of their preferred ways of articulating this distinction entails (or strongly supports) the thesis that actions contrary to the agent's *J* are unfree. Now, Watson is a compatibilist proponent of *UF*, but I have shown that his argument for *UF* is unpersuasive. In general, compatibilists, like most philosophers, do not reject the possibility of core weak-willed action. Any stronger arguments than Watson's for *UF* that may be forthcoming from compatibilists would also deserve attention.

Obviously, the many extant versions of compatibilism and libertarianism cannot be reviewed here, but two general points can be made. First, if a view of free action entails that all intentional actions contrary to the agent's *J* are unfree, that itself would provide grounds to be suspicious of the view. Of course, if the view were to hold up under examination, we would have grounds for rejecting the common-sense view that there are core weak-willed actions. Second, unless proponents of UF produce a convincing argument for the no-matter-what thesis, they have the burden of defending a position on free action and arguing for *UF* in light of that position or, alternatively, of showing that only a certain range of positions on free action have a chance of being true and arguing for *UF* in light of some fact about that range. These projects are challenging.

3. Compatibilist and Libertarian Resources

In the present section, I sketch some compatibilist and libertarian ways of distinguishing between compelled and weak-willed action contrary to one's *J*. My aim is to display some of the resources believers in free action have at their disposal in developing a distinction.

John Fischer and Mark Ravizza defend the thesis that "an agent is morally responsible for an action insofar as it issues from his own, moderately reasons-responsive mechanism" (1998, p. 86). The same can be said of an agent's performing an action freely. An agent makes a mechanism his own by "taking responsibility" for it. "Moderate reasons-responsiveness consists in *regular reasons-receptivity*, and at least *weak reasons-reactivity*, of the actual-sequence mechanism that leads to the action" (p. 89; italics added). Reasons-receptivity is "the capacity to recognize the reasons that exist," and reasons-reactivity is "the capacity to translate reasons into choices (and then subsequent behavior)" (p. 69). "It is a defining characteristic of *regular* reasons-receptivity that it involves an understandable pattern of (actual and hypothetical) reasons-receptivity" (p. 71; italics added). A mechanism of an agent that issues in the agent's *A*-ing in the actual world is at least *weakly* reasons-reactive provided that there is some possible world with the same laws in which a mechanism of this kind is operative in this agent, "there is a sufficient reason to do otherwise, the agent recognizes this reason, and the agent does otherwise" (p. 63) for this reason.

It may be suggested that core weak-willed action differs from compelled action contrary to one's *J* in that whereas weak-willed action "issues from [the agent's] own, moderately reasons-responsive mechanism," compelled action does not. Although, in both scenarios, agents may satisfy the conditions for regular reasons-receptivity, the mechanism of the agent who acts in a weak-willed way "is at least weakly reasons-reactive" and the compelled agent's mechanism is not. In the case of the latter agent, there is no world of the specified sort in which he "does otherwise." It may be said that this, indeed, is precisely what it is for a desire to be irresistible and, hence, to have compelling force.

Elsewhere, I have argued that weak reasons-reactivity is too weak to do the work that Fischer and Ravizza want it to do for moral responsibility (2000b).[13] The objection advanced there bears on the present issue as well. Even in extreme cases of phobia or addiction *some* reason usually can be imagined such that if the agent, who *A*-ed owing significantly to his phobia or addiction, had had that reason for *B*-ing, he would have *B*-ed for that reason rather than *A*-ing. Bearing in mind that an agent's relevant mechanism's reacting positively, in a possible world, to a good reason for *B*-ing is sufficient for weak reasons-reactivity on Fischer and Ravizza's view, consider the following case (from Mele 1992a, p. 87). Fred's agoraphobia is so powerful that he has not ventured out of his house in ten years, despite his family's many attempts to persuade him to do so and the many incentives they have offered him. Owing to his fear, he often has decided not to do things that he believed he had good reason to do and that he judged it would be best to do (and then behaved in accordance with his decision). For example, he recently decided to stay at home (and stayed there) rather than leave his house on his beloved daughter's wedding day. She was married in the church next door. Fred believed that he had good reason to attend the wedding, believed, accordingly, that he had good reason to leave his house, and judged that it would best to leave his house. Now, in some possible world with the same laws, there was a raging fire in Fred's house that day. Fred is even more afraid of raging fires than of leaving his house. In this possible world, he judged that he had a good reason to leave his house, and he decided to do so, for that reason. Fred left his house, walked next door, and, making a heroic effort, entered the church.

Fred's relevant mechanism is weakly reasons-reactive. We can suppose that it is also regularly reasons-receptive and that it is Fred's own mechanism. (Nothing in Fred's story precludes this.) Thus, on Fischer and Ravizza's view, Fred is morally responsible for staying at home on his daughter's wedding day (in the actual world), and on the view at issue about weak-willed action, Fred exhibits weakness of will in staying home. However, this is implausible. Other things being equal (for example, Fred is not morally responsible for his agoraphobia), if Fred's fear is so debilitating that it would take something as frightening as a raging fire to move him to decide to leave his house or to leave it intentionally, then he seems *not* to be morally responsible for staying home. Similarly, the problem he manifests in staying home on his daughter's wedding day seems much more severe than weakness of will.

If things are as they seem to be, then the suggested distinction between core weak-willed action and compelled action against one's *J* is untenable. However, semicompatibilists certainly have room to maneuver, as I have observed elsewhere (Mele 2006a, pp. 151–52, 2006b, p. 290). Fischer and Ravizza's appeal to moderate reasons-responsiveness is motivated partly by a problem with Fischer's earlier "weak reasons-responsiveness" view (1994). Perhaps additional refinements will accomplish the present trick. In *Springs of Action* (1992a, ch. 5), in the course of constructing an analysis of irresistible desire, I argue that an agent's desire to A (for example, to stay home) may properly count as irresistible even if he would successfully resist it in some extreme counterfactual scenarios. (Philosophers averse to using "irresistible desire" in this way may be less resistant to a comparable use of "compelling desire" or "desire with compelling force.") Semicompatibilists who were to be persuaded of this might find a principled way of motivating a reasons-reactivity constraint on free action that is moderately stronger than weak reasons-reactivity.[14] Of course, the boundary (if there is one) between compelled action contrary to one's J and core weak-willed action may be fuzzy, but constraints on free action can be comparably fuzzy.

It is easy to imagine a traditional compatibilist analogue of a semicompatibilist distinction between core weak-willed action and compelled action against one's J. A bit of background will help explain why. What separates semicompatibilists from traditional compatibilists is a disagreement about "could have done otherwise." According to a standard incompatibilist view, an agent who A-ed at t was able to do otherwise at t only if in another possible world with the same past and laws of nature as his world, he does otherwise at t. Obviously, an agent whose world is deterministic could never have done otherwise than he did, on this reading of "could have done otherwise." Traditional compatibilists and semicompatibilists agree that freely A-ing does not require that the agent could have done otherwise than A in this sense. They disagree about a related issue. The former hold that there is a "could have done otherwise" requirement on free action and moral responsibility, and they endeavor to develop one that is compatible with determinism; the latter hold that free action and moral responsibility are compatible with determinism even if determinism is incompatible with its ever being the case that an agent could have done otherwise. In response to a traditional compatibilist's proposed account of the "could have done otherwise" requirement—an account intended to specify something such that if all the other conditions for freedom and moral responsibility with respect to his *A*-ing are satisfied by an agent, adding satisfaction of this condition to the mix renders the action free and one for which the agent is morally responsible—semicompatibilists can side with incompatibilists in arguing that the account is not of something that deserves the label "could have done otherwise." If a semicompatibilist were to accept the proposed account (as intended by its proponents) and to agree that determinism is compatible with its being true that agents could have done otherwise in that sense, "semi" should be dropped from the name of his or her view.

Traditional compatibilists who regard some Frankfurt-style cases as coherent can consistently claim that there is a sense in which the featured agents could have done otherwise that is crucial for freedom and moral responsibility. Like semicompatibilists, they can tie free action and moral responsibility to reasons-responsiveness and understand the latter in terms of reasons-receptivity and reasons-reactivity. Part of their disagreement with semicompatibilists is about the possible worlds relevant for tests of these capacities. Some traditional compatibilists may claim that "counterfactual controllers" are absent from relevant possible worlds in Frankfurt-style cases, on the grounds that the potential controller's plans and powers are irrelevant to the agent's pertinent capacities or abilities, properly understood: the counterfactual controllers may simply mask the agent's actual abilities (Smith 1997). Traditional compatibilists are, in principle, in a position to advance views of reasons-responsiveness and its connection to free action and moral responsibility that differ from semicompatibilist views mainly in asserting that this reasons-responsiveness is sufficient for "could have done otherwise." Traditional compatibilist views along these lines may yield accounts of the difference between compelled action against the agent's *J* and core weak-willed action that are every bit as subtle as accounts that semicompatibilists are in a position to offer (see Smith 2003).

Libertarians have a variety of resources for distinguishing core weak-willed action from compelled action against the agent's *J*. If there can be instances of local deterministic causation in indeterministic worlds, libertarians can claim that compelled action differs from core weak-willed action in being deterministically caused. Libertarian accounts of free action and moral responsibility can, and often do, feature reasons-responsiveness. The main difference, in this regard, between libertarians and compatibilists (including semicompatibilists) is that the former alone maintain that freedom- and responsibility-level reasons-responsiveness requires that the agent "could have done otherwise" on a determinism-precluding reading of that expression.

Some philosophers who believe that we sometimes act freely may find that they are not persuaded by any extant libertarian or compatibilist (including semicompatibilist) proposal for distinguishing compelled or otherwise unfree action contrary to the agent's *J* from core weak-willed action. This might incline them to believe that there are no core weak-willed actions. But an alternative option for belief is certainly alive and kicking—namely, that if one were to encounter a detailed, persuasive view of free action, it would encompass or yield a persuasive account of the difference between actions of these two kinds. Dissatisfaction with extant accounts of free action is one thing; having grounds for believing that there are no core weak-willed actions even though one believes that some intentional actions are free (*P1*) and that some intentional actions are contrary to the agent's *J* (*P2*) is another.

I remarked that proponents of *UF* have their work cut out for them. Of course, philosophers who reject *UF* and claim, with lay folk, that core weak-willed action is possible have work to do too. A thorough job would include defending an account of free action (including deciding freely)—a major undertaking—and showing that it is consistent with core weak-willed action. I cannot do that in this book. (Again, I develop two detailed accounts of free action in *Free Will and Luck* (2006a)—one for compatibilists and the other for libertarians.) But I do hope to have shown that worries from believers in free action that alleged weak-willed actions are indistinguishable from compelled actions are seriously inflated. It might turn out that, on a particular view of free action, the distinction cannot be made, but what accounts for that may be that that view of free action is false.

FOUR

• • •

Accounting for Backsliding: Background and More

I have defined *core weak-willed* action as free, sane, intentional action that, as the nondepressed agent consciously recognizes at the time of action, is contrary to his better judgment, a judgment based on practical reasoning. If there are any such actions, how is their occurrence to be accounted for? This conditional question guides the present chapter. I sketch a theoretical and empirical framework that sheds light on how the occurrence of core weak-willed actions may be accounted for *if* they occur, and I apply that framework to an apparent instance of core weak-willed action.

1. Better Judgment*

R. M. Hare claims that "moral judgments, in their central use, have it as their function to guide conduct" (1963, p. 70). A related claim about agents' *better judgments* is plausible—namely, that their primary function is to guide conduct. Again, the contents of better judgments, as I conceive of them, are declarative propositions. A theorist who doubts that assent to a declarative proposition can guide conduct—for example, the proposition that it would be best on the whole to study all evening for tomorrow's test—may seek an alternative notion of better judgment. Avoiding a radical departure from most of the traditional literature on weak-willed action requires retaining the idea that better judgments have truth-valued content. But this leaves open, for example, the proposal that more is essential to a proper notion of better judgment than assent to declarative propositions of a certain kind. In this section, I discuss a version of this proposal to set part of the stage for discussion of a view according to which better judgments are not only well suited to guide conduct but also are subject to defeat in instances of core weak-willed action. The alternative proposal about better judgments to be discussed and rejected here may be used in an attempt to support the thesis that core weak-willed actions are impossible.

A pair of distinctions will prove useful. Some better judgments are about what it is best to do now, and others are about what it is best to do later. Ann may judge that it is best to interrupt an offensive speaker now, and Bob may judge that it is best to leave for the airport an hour from now. Better judgments of these kinds may be termed, respectively, *proximal* and *distal* better judgments. There are also proximal and distal intentions (Mele 1992a, 2009, pp. 10–11). If Ann has an intention to interrupt the speaker now, it is a proximal intention; and if Bob has an intention to leave for the airport an hour from now, it is a distal intention.

Suppose someone were to claim that when an agent is deliberating about what to do now, anything that deserves the label "better judgment" is, by definition, a conscious judgment to the effect that it is best to A now that is paired with a conscious proximal intention to A. Pairs of these kinds may be termed *better judgments**. The presence of a conscious proximal intention does not ensure its successful execution—or even an attempt. Someone who consciously proximally intends to answer his phone may be distracted by a gunshot outside his window—or, alternatively, be shot to death—even before he has time to begin reaching for the phone. Also, if a story like Alex's in chapter 3 (section 1) is possible, someone who has a conscious proximal intention to cut himself as part of a ceremony may, owing to a natural (but defeasible) aversion, intentionally stop short; the former intention may be supplanted by an effective intention to stop.[1] However, if an agent cannot intentionally refrain from A-ing *while* he has a conscious proximal intention to A, Alex cannot intentionally refrain from cutting himself while his conscious proximal intention to cut himself remains in place.[2] If that is right, then if Alex judges it best to cut himself now—given the definition of "better judgment" under consideration—intentional behavior contrary to the judgment is not open to him as long as the judgment stands, because the continued presence of the judgment requires the continued presence of a conscious proximal intention to cut himself. This would distinguish better judgments* from any alleged conscious better judgments whose presence throughout a span of time t does not preclude weak-willed behavior against them during t.

Perhaps I have identified a kind of better judgment—better judgment*—so constituted that, as long as it persists, weak-willed behavior against it is not open to the agent. However, because the intention built into better judgment* is doing the work, the notion is not likely to evoke enthusiasm. A better judgment* is just a better judgment (on a familiar reading of "judgment") about what to do now *plus* a corresponding conscious intention; it is an artificial construction out of a pair of mental items.

Fortunately, we do not need to suppose that the better judgments involved in alleged cases of core weak-willed action are better judgments* in order to find core weak-willed action theoretically challenging. Imagine that, on the basis of careful deliberation about whether to stay in and study tonight or instead attend a friend's party, Jack consciously and rationally judges it best on the whole to spend the entire evening studying for tomorrow's test. Imagine also, if you can, that Jack intentionally goes to the party and intentionally does not study and that, as he is leaving his apartment for the party, he is aware that what he is doing is contrary to his current better judgment. Jack's judgment is made from the perspective of his own values and beliefs; and he values, among other things, doing well in school, getting a good grade on the test, having fun, and spending time with friends. How can the desires that motivate Jack to attend the party (for example, his desire to have fun tonight and his desire to see friends tonight) win out, given that he took them into account in arriving at his judgment? There are glib answers: well, no one is perfect. But something more substantial would be nice.

In effect, Jack judged that it would be better to satisfy the desires that support his studying all evening than the desires that support his attending the party instead. How can it happen that despite this judgment (and in the absence of insanity and depression), Jack intentionally and freely goes to the party while consciously recognizing that doing so is contrary to his better judgment? This, I take it, is an interesting question. And the question is more interesting than it would be if we were to know that better judgments, by their very nature, preclude core weak-willed actions against them, because then we would know both that and why the correct answer to the question about Jack is *This cannot happen*.

Core weak-willed action does not depend for its being theoretically challenging on the supposition that the better judgments at issue are actually better judgments*. In section 3, I explain why better judgments do not depend for their being fit to function as action guides on their being better judgments*.

2. Two Perspectives on Intentional Action

Both philosophical and lay thinking about action include a pair of perspectives on the explanation of intentional actions, a *motivational* and an *intellectual* one. Central to the motivational perspective is the idea that what agents do when they act intentionally is tightly linked to what they are most strongly motivated to do at the time. This perspective is taken on *all* intentional actions, independently of the biological species to which the agents belong. If, for instance, cats, dogs, and human beings act intentionally, the motivational perspective has all three species in its sights. Those who adopt the motivational perspective believe that, in the case of intentional actions, information about why agents were in the motivational condition they were in at the time of action contributes to our understanding of why they acted as they did. Although it is sometimes assumed that the connection between what agents are most strongly motivated to do at a time and what they try to do at that time is deterministic, a notion of motivational strength does not need to presuppose determinism (neither global determinism nor local determinism about the internal workings of agents). This is a source of comfort to any libertarians inclined to believe that some desires have more motivational strength than others (see Clarke 1994). Even if Ann's desire to strike an offensive person is stronger than her desire to walk away instead, it may be open to her to do the latter. Whether this is open depends on what else is true of her. Perhaps an agent can resist a stronger desire and act on a weaker one, and perhaps the connection between desires and actions is indeterministic in such a way that there is only a probability (less than 1) that one will act on the stronger of two competing desires for action if one acts on either. (For an articulation and a defense of a notion of motivational strength, see Mele 2003, chs. 7 and 8.)

The intellectual perspective applies only to intellectual beings. Whatever the minimally sufficient conditions for inclusion in the class of intellectual beings may be, practical intellect, as it is normally conceived, is concerned (among other things) with weighing options and making judgments about what it is best, better, or good enough to do. Central to the intellectual perspective is the idea that such judgments play a significant role in explaining some intentional actions of intellectual beings.

Many philosophers have sought to combine these two perspectives into one in the domain of intentional human action. One tack is to insist that, in intellectual beings, motivational strength and evaluative judgment always travel hand in hand. Socrates is commonly interpreted as advancing this view in connection with his contention that no one ever knowingly does wrong (Plato, *Protagoras* 352b–358d). Theorists who take this tack have several options. For example, they can hold that judgment (causally or conceptually) determines motivational strength, that motivational strength (causally or conceptually) determines judgment, or that judgment and motivational strength have a common determinant.

The apparent occurrence of core weak-willed actions constitutes a problem for this general tack. The motivational perspective is well suited to weak-willed action: when agents perform weak-willed actions, they presumably (at least ordinarily) do what they are most strongly motivated to do at the time. But the intellectual perspective is threatened by the apparent occurrence of actions of this kind: more precisely, certain interpretations of—or theses about—that perspective are challenged. In threatening the intellectual perspective while leaving the motivational perspective unchallenged, the apparent occurrence of core weak-willed actions poses apparent difficulties for the project of combining the two perspectives into a unified outlook on the explanation of intentional human actions. That is a primary source of perennial philosophical interest in core weak-willed action.

It is no accident that the motivational and intellectual perspectives have evolved and survived. They seem to help make sense of our intentional behavior, and a plausible combination is theoretically desirable. To some theorists, the threat that core weak-willed action poses to a unified, motivational/ intellectual perspective has seemed so severe that they have rejected such action as logically or psychologically impossible

(Hare 1963, ch. 5). Many others have sought to accommodate core weak-willed action in a unified perspective.

A proper account of the two perspectives must mention various alleged intermediaries between motivation and judgment on the one hand and overt intentional action on the other—decision (or choice) and intention, in particular. These items are featured in various versions of *both* perspectives, a fact that may be taken as grounds for hope that the perspectives may be plausibly combined. The motivational and intellectual perspectives on the explanation of intentional human action converge not only on overt intentional action but also on decision and intention. (To decide to *A*, as I understand practical deciding, is to perform a momentary mental action of forming an intention to *A*. Deciding, so construed, is a nonovert species of intentional action. See Mele 2003, ch. 9.)

Aristotle claimed that choice (*prohairesis*), "the origin of action—its efficient, not its final cause," is "either desiderative reason [*orektikos nous*] or ratiocinative desire [*orexis dianoetike*]" (*Nicomachean Ethics* 1139a31–32, 1139b4–5). On one reading, Aristotle could not make up his mind whether choice belongs to the genus *judgment* or the genus *motivation*. On another reading, choice is a hybrid: it is judgment together with relevant motivation, and perhaps judgment together with proportional relevant motivation.[3] Donald Davidson (1980, ch. 5, 1985b, p. 206) holds, in a similar vein, that an "unconditional" better judgment is an *intention*; and R. M. Hare (1963, p. 79), as I understand him, maintains that assenting to a "value-judgment" that one ought to *X* entails *intending* to *X* (in the guise of assenting "to the command 'Let me do *X*'").

In *Autonomous Agents* (1995, ch. 2), I argue that Aristotle, Davidson, and Hare do not provide "good grounds for holding that some nonartificially construed . . . judgments are by their very nature (as opposed to nature plus accompanying circumstances) akrasia-proof" (p. 25), and I motivate an alternative view of the connection between better judgments and intentions. I do not reproduce those arguments here; but in the following section I sketch the alternative view, focusing on better judgments produced by practical evaluative reasoning.

3. Practical Evaluative Reasoning

Practical evaluative reasoning, as I understand it, is a cognitive process that involves some evaluative premises and is driven at least partly by motivation to settle on what to do (Mele 1992a, ch. 12, 1995, ch. 2).[4] This motivation disposes agents to intend in accordance with the reasoning's evaluative conclusion. Their being so disposed supports the primary purpose of practical evaluative reasoning, which is to lead to a satisfactory *resolution* of one's practical problem. An agent who judges it best to *A* but is still unsettled about whether to *A* has not resolved his practical problem. (Recall the story about Joe the smoker in chapter 2.) The agent's forming or acquiring an intention to *A* would settle matters.

In my view, a common route from an *A*-favoring better judgment produced by practical evaluative reasoning to an intention to *A* is a *default* route (Mele 1992a, ch. 12). Consider *default* procedures in computing—for example, a standard procedure in common word-processing programs for the spacing of text. When authors create new files, any text they type will be displayed single-spaced, unless they preempt this default condition of creating a file by entering a command for an alternative form of spacing. When authors do not issue a preemptive command and their programs and hardware are working properly, entering a new file systematically has the identified result. Similarly, in the absence of preemptive conditions (for example, strong opposing desires) in normally functioning human beings, their judging it best to *A* might systematically issue in an intention to *A*. Forming a better judgment in favor of *A*-ing might figure importantly in the production of an intention to *A* in particular cases, even if the transition from such judgments to such intentions sometimes is blocked—even if the disposition to make that transition is defeasible.

The basic idea is that "normal human agents are so constituted that, in the absence of preemption, judging it best . . . to *A* issues directly in the acquisition of an intention to *A*" (Mele 1992a, p. 231). In simple cases involving little or no motivational opposition, the transition from judgment to intention is smooth and easy. In such cases, agents who judge it best to *A* have no need to think about whether to intend to *A*; nor, given their motivational condition, do they need to exercise self-control in order to bring it about that they intend to *A*. No special intervening effort of any sort is required. The existence of a default procedure of the sort at issue in normal human agents would help explain the smoothness and ease of the transition. Indeed, we should expect an efficient action-directed system in beings who are capable both of making deliberative judgments and of performing weak-willed actions to encompass such a procedure. Special energy should be exerted in this connection only when one's better judgments encounter significant opposition.[5] If and when there is a weak-willed failure to intend in accordance with one's better judgments, opposition is encountered: something blocks a default transition; something preempts the default value of the judgment.

In *Springs of Action* (1992a, pp. 230–34), I distinguish among three kinds of case in which an agent's better judgment is opposed by competing motivation: (1) a default process unproblematically generates a judgment-matching intention even in the face of the opposition; (2) a judgment-matching intention is formed even though the default route to intention is blocked by the opposition; (3) the motivational opposition blocks the default route to intention and figures in the production of a weak-willed intention. What is needed is a principled way of carving up the territory. In the same book, I suggest that a judgment-matching intention is produced (in the normal way) by default, as opposed to being produced via a distinct causal route, when and only when (barring causal overdetermination, the assistance of other agents, science fiction, and the like) no intervening exercise of *self-control* contributes to the production of the intention (p. 233). (Sometimes opposing motivation is sufficiently weak that no attempt at self-control is called for.) If the move from better judgment to intention does not involve a special intervening effort on the agent's part, the intention's presence typically may safely be attributed to the operation of a default procedure.

In my view, self-control also has a place in explanations of why, when a default route from better judgment to intention *is* blocked, we sometimes do and sometimes do not intend on the basis of our better judgments. Barring the operation of higher-order default processes, overdetermination, interference by intention-producing demons, and so on, whether an agent intends in accordance with his better judgment in such cases depends on his own efforts at self-control. In simple cases of self-indulgence (see the story about Mike the tourist in chapter 2), the agent makes no effort at all to perform the action judged best, or to form the appropriate intention. In other cases in which an agent judges it best to A, he might attempt in any number of ways to get himself to A or to intend to A. He might try focusing his attention on the desirable results of his A-ing or on the unattractive aspects of his not A-ing. He might generate vivid images of both, or utter self-commands. If all else fails, he might seek help from a behavioral therapist. Whether his strategies work will depend on the details of the case; but strategies such as these *can* have a salutary effect, as empirical research on delay of gratification and behavior control amply indicates.[6]

Why do we reason about what it would be best to do? Sometimes, at least, because we are concerned to *do* what it would be best to do and have not yet identified what that is. (Often, we may settle—even rationally settle—on the first alternative that strikes us as good enough: for example, when we take little to be at stake and suppose that the cost required to identify the best alternative would probably outweigh the benefits.) In such cases, if things go smoothly, better judgments issue in corresponding intentions. And it is no accident that they do, given what motivates the reasoning that issues in the judgments.

Of course, if common sense can be trusted, things do not *always* go smoothly: we can identify the better and—owing partly to the influence of recalcitrant desires—intend the worse. If this happens, the fact that it does would show, not that better judgments have no role to play in the etiology of intentions and intentional behavior, but rather that, in human beings as they actually are, an agent's judging it best to A does not ensure that he forms or acquires a corresponding intention. In *Irrationality* (1987), I attempt to explain *how* this can be true, how better judgments may be rendered ineffective by competing motivation. My positive aim in this section has been to sketch a view according to which (1) the assumption that it *is* true is compatible with better judgments' having an important role to play in the production of intentions and, hence, intentional actions, and (2) their playing such a role in no way depends on there being a nonartificial, *akrasia*-proof species of better judgment. Once one sees that the capacity of better judgments to play a significant role in the production of intentional actions does not depend on the existence of a nonartificial, *akrasia*-proof variety of better judgment, one may be less inclined to suppose that there is such a species.

It is tempting to speculate about how a default procedure of the sort that I have sketched might have emerged in us. Any speculation about how agents like us come about— agents who sometimes reason about what it would be best to do with a view to settling on what *to* do and then intend and act on the basis of their better judgments—should attend to the emergence in such agents of what mediates between judgment and action. Agents like us would be well served by a default procedure of the kind sketched: a procedure of this kind conserves mental energy, obviating a need for a special effort or act, in each case, to bring it about that, having judged it best to A, one also intends to A. Special efforts would be required only in special circumstances. I have suggested that we *are* served by a procedure of this kind and that, because we are, there is no need for an *akrasia*-proof species of better judgment in an acceptable theory of the connection between practical evaluative thought and intentional action.

4. Desire and Motivation

I wrote a book on motivation: *Motivation and Agency* (2003). In it, I develop interlocking conceptions of motivation and desire. Fortunately, not all the details are needed for the purposes of the present book, but enough should be said to give readers a sense of how I conceive of an important species of desire.

Richard Peters concludes *The Concept of Motivation* by chiding motivational psychologists for their scientific aspirations and suggesting that "scrutiny of the conceptually illuminating start made by Aristotle" would provide a more promising approach (1958, p. 157). One of the chief faults that Peters finds with motivational psychologists is their commitment to a *causal* approach to explaining behavior. When he wrote his conclusion, Peters seemingly forgot a striking claim in book 6 of Aristotle's *Nicomachean Ethics*: "the origin of action—its efficient, not its final cause—is choice, and that of choice is desire and reasoning with a view to an end" (1139a31–32).

The term "orexis," translated here as "desire," also may be translated as "motivation." One reason that "desire" is more convenient than "motivation" as a standard translation for "orexis" is that it allows more easily for the precise specification of the *object* of a motivation-encompassing attitude—that is, of what is desired. Another is that the noun "orexis" has a cognate verb, "orego," and both can be translated as "desire," but not, of course, as "motivation." Setting classical Greek aside, related points may be made about philosophical uses of the terms "desire," "want," and "motivation." We can say that someone desires to swim today, or, more naturally, that she wants to swim today; and we can say that someone has a desire to swim today, or, less naturally, that she has a want to swim today. However, the expressions "is motivated to swim today" and "has motivation to swim today" are not only more awkward than their most elegant counterpart, they are also less precise. Suppose that Ann wants to swim today because she wants to exercise today (as she does every day) and believes that, given a tendon injury sustained in her daily running, swimming currently is the best form of exercise for her. Then Ann is motivated to swim today, in the sense that she has motivation to swim today, and some speakers find it natural to say that the attitudes motivating her to swim today include both her desire to exercise today and her desire to swim today. The assertions that Ann is motivated to swim today and that she has motivation to swim today do not, at least in some idiolects, distinguish between these two motivation-encompassing attitudes.

Partly for reasons of precision, some philosophers have adopted the convention of using the noun "desire," or "want," as a synonym for "motivation" in some contexts. This practice, which I find useful, occasionally troubles aficionados of ordinary usage. "Desire" brings to mind affective tone or appetitive content, and "has a want to A" is stilted. These worries can be quelled. As I noted elsewhere (Mele 1992a, p. 47, following Goldman 1970, pp. 53–54), distinctions blurred by this usage can be recaptured by differentiating among types of wants or desires (which terms may be used interchangeably as terms of art). For example, one can distinguish egoistic from altruistic desires, affective from nonaffective desires, and appetitive from nonappetitive desires (compare my desire to drink a pint of Guinness with your desire to continue reading this chapter).

Ann's desire to exercise today, her desire to swim today, and my desire to shoot pool with Jason tomorrow are *action-desires*, desires to act in certain ways. Action-desires are paradigmatic motivational attitudes. What are they motivation for, or motivation to do? At the very least, desires to A, where A is a prospective course of action, constitute motivation to A. For example, Ann's desire to exercise today constitutes motivation to exercise today, and my desire to shoot pool with Jason tomorrow constitutes motivation to shoot pool with Jason tomorrow.

Action-desires, as I understand them, are important members of the class of essentially motivation-encompassing attitudes. Readers interested in an analysis of such attitudes—a complicated one, unfortunately—may consult chapter 6 of Mele (2003). An important feature of these attitudes is that they have (roughly) the function of contributing to their own satisfaction by inducing the agent to act on them.

In *Motivation and Agency*, I identified the following six popular theses in the philosophical and psychological literature on motivation.

1. Motivation is present in the animal kingdom but does not extend throughout it.[7]
2. Motivated beings have a capacity to represent goals and means to goals.
3. A motivation-encompassing attitude may have either a goal or a means as its object.
4. Motivation varies in strength.
5. The stronger an agent's motivation to A is, in comparison to the agent's motivation for alternative courses of

action, the more likely the agent is to *A*, other things being equal.⁸
6. Whenever agents act intentionally, there is something they are effectively motivated to do.⁹ (2003, p. 3)

My concern in that book is a notion of motivation consistent with (among other things) these six claims. I accept each of these claims along with parallel claims about action-desires and beings that have them.

Naturally, I criticized some alternative views of desire in *Motivation and Agency*. Here I repeat my brief criticism of one such view (see pp. 78–79), because the view seems to be gaining popularity in some circles.

T. M. Scanlon offers an account of "what is usually called desire" (1998, p. 65). He contends that something's seeming to an agent to be a reason for *A*-ing is "the central element in what is usually called [a] desire" to *A* (p. 65). Seemings of this kind do important motivational work, according to Scanlon. He claims that in a thirsty man with a desire to drink, "the motivational work seems to be done by" the agent's taking "the pleasure to be obtained by drinking . . . to count in favor of drinking" (p. 38).

Scanlon's account of what is usually called a desire is overly intellectualized. It is generally granted that toddlers and pre-toddlers desire to do things—for example, to drink some juice or to hug a teddy bear. This common thought is not that although these little agents desire to do things, they lack "what is usually called a desire." The thought is that they have desires in a normal, "usual" sense of the term. But because it is unlikely that toddlers have the concept of a reason for action (or of something's counting in favor of a course of action), it is unlikely that things seem to them to be reasons for action (or to count in favor of actions). There is considerable evidence that younger three-year-olds tend not to have the concept, or a proper concept, of belief and that, although the concept of desire emerges earlier, it does not emerge until around the age of two (see Gopnik 1993 for a review). Presumably, even if the concept of a reason for action were to have no conceptual ties to the concepts of belief and desire, it would be sufficiently sophisticated to be out of reach of children too young to have proper concepts of belief and desire. Even so, such children sometimes act intentionally and for reasons. So, at least, it is commonly and plausibly thought. (They also are commonly thought to have desires and beliefs. Not many theorists hold that having such attitudes requires possessing concepts of these attitudes.)[10] In the case of a thirsty toddler or pretoddler, a desire to drink—rather than any taking of "the pleasure to be obtained by drinking" to be a reason for drinking—seems to do the work of motivating drinking.

To be attracted by the prospect of drinking is one thing; to take an anticipated consequence of drinking to be a reason for (or "count in favor of") drinking is another. Thirsty toddlers are attracted by cups of juice, and not in the way moths are attracted by light. Toddlers are flexible in their approach to getting drinks: they try alternative means.[11] Moths behave tropistically. Even though it is unlikely that thirsty toddlers have the conceptual wherewithal to take features, including anticipated consequences, of drinking to be reasons for (or "count in favor of") drinking, they are attracted by cups of juice in a way characteristic of desiring agents. Being attracted to cups of juice owing to a sensitivity to certain of their features is distinguishable from being attracted to cups of juice owing to the agent's taking these features to be reasons. An agent's behavior may be sensitive to attractive features of things without the agent's taking those features to be reasons. If this were not so, a radically new theory of animal behavior would be required, one entailing either that only members of the most conceptually sophisticated species perform actions (perhaps just human beings) or that many nonhuman species are much more conceptually sophisticated than anyone has thought.

When ordinary thirsty adults drink (intentionally, and in ordinary scenarios), they presumably are motivated at least partly by a desire to drink. The strength of the desire may sometimes be explained partly by their believing that drinking would be pleasant, or, more fully, by that belief together with a desire for pleasure. A toddler's desire to drink water and an adult's desire to drink water may admit of the same analysis. Just as something's seeming to be a reason for drinking is not a constituent of the toddler's desire, it might not be a constituent of the adult's desire either. If a seeming of this kind sometimes is at work in thirsty adults, it may function as a partial cause of the desire's strength or of the desire itself.

5. Accounting for Core Weak-Willed Action: A Sketch

In *Irrationality* (1987), I defend a view about what happens in cases of core weak-willed action. I sketch the view in the present section and develop it more fully later. My view rests partly on the following two theses and on various arguments for these theses.

> T1. Our better judgments normally are based at least partly on our evaluations of objects of our desires (that is, desired items).
>
> T2. The motivational strength of our desires does not always match our evaluations of the objects of our desires.

If both theses are true, it should be unsurprising that sometimes, although we judge it best to *A* and better to *A* than to *B*, we are more strongly motivated to *B* than to *A*. Given how our motivation stacks up on these occasions, it should also be unsurprising that we *B* rather than *A*.

Thesis *T1* is a major plank in a standard conception of practical reasoning. In general, when we reason about what to do, we try to figure out what it would be best, better, or good enough to do, not what we are most strongly motivated to do. When we engage in such reasoning while having relevant conflicting desires, our concluding judgments typically are based partly on our assessments of the objects of those desires—which may be out of line with the motivational strength of those desires, if *T2* is true.

Thesis *T2* is confirmed by common experience and thought experiments (see Mele 1987, pp. 37–39), and it has a foundation in empirical studies. As I will explain, influences on desire strength are not limited to evaluations of the objects of desires, and other factors that influence desire strength may fail to have a matching effect on assessments of desired objects.

One should not have to work hard to persuade readers of the truth of *T2*. Recall the story about agoraphobic Fred (chapter 3, section 3). If the strengths of his pertinent desires (including his desire to go to the wedding and his desire to stay home) had matched his evaluations of the objects of those desires, he would have been more strongly motivated to attend the wedding, as he judged best, than to stay in his house, and he very probably would have walked to the wedding at the church next door. Similarly, as I observe in *Irrationality*, someone with a severe fear of flying may judge it best to board a plane now (because it is the only way to get to an important job interview) and yet be so anxious about flying that he does not board the plane (p. 37). If the strengths of his desires had matched his evaluations of the objects of those desires, he very probably would have boarded the plane. In the case of actions of the kinds at issue, an agent's both judging it best to A and being preponderantly motivated to A makes it very likely that he will A. I also offer the following far-fetched scenario in *Irrationality* for any readers inclined to think that it is a necessary truth that the motivational strength of a desire always matches the agent's evaluation of the desire's object:

> Imagine that an evil genius is able to implant and directly maintain very strong desires in people, and that he does this to Susan. However, because she knows both that her desire to

A was produced by the evil genius and that he does this sort of thing solely with a view to getting those in whom the desires are implanted to destroy themselves, Susan gives her *A*-ing a very low evaluative ranking. She believes that her not *A*-ing would be much better, all things considered. Nevertheless, the genius's control over the strength of Susan's desire to do *A* is such that the balance of her motivation falls on the side of her *A*-ing. (pp. 37–38)

Though the scenario is far-fetched, it certainly seems conceptually possible.

If we were *ideal* agents, our evaluations of the objects of our desires might always determine and be matched by the strength of those desires. If we were agents like that and we ranked quitting smoking higher than smoking our next cigarette, studying now higher than playing video games now, forgoing an after-dinner snack higher than eating one, and so on, our desires for the more highly ranked conduct would be stronger than our competing desires, and acting as we judged best would be easy. But there is lots of evidence that we are not ideal agents of this kind. If we were, there would be no market for self-help books that focus on strategies for resisting temptation. Such resistance would be a piece of cake: we would always be most strongly motivated to do what we judge best.

George Ainslie makes a powerful case for the thesis that the motivational strength of desires tends to increase hyperbolically as the time for their satisfaction approaches (1992, 2001). If there is not a matching tendency in our evaluations of the objects of our desires, it may often happen that the strength of a desire is seriously out of line with the agent's assessment of its object. When a dieter, Dan, is perusing his dinner menu, he may give eating dessert later a low evaluation, judge it best to skip dessert, and have a desire of moderate strength for an after-dinner dessert. But when the dessert menu is delivered to his table after he has finished his low-calorie meal, the strength of his desire may spike dramatically, as predicted by Ainslie's model (discussed in chapter 5). If this happens without his assessment of the goodness of eating dessert also spiking dramatically, we have motivation-evaluation misalignment, and Dan may judge it best not to order dessert while being more strongly motivated to order it than not to order it. In section 7, I explain how this can happen.

Empirical studies of the role of representations of desired objects in impulsive behavior and delay of gratification (reviewed in Mele 1987 and 1995 and discussed in section 6) provide powerful evidence that our representations of desired objects have two important dimensions, a motivational and an informational one. Our better judgments may be more sensitive to the informational dimension of our representations than to the motivational dimension, with the result that such judgments sometimes recommend actions that are out of line with what we are most strongly motivated to do at the time. If so, core weak-willed action is a real possibility—provided that at least some intentional actions that conflict with our reasoned better judgments are freely and sanely performed in the absence of depression. To be sure, some philosophers have argued that none of our actions that conflict with our better judgments can be free; but as I explained in chapter 3, the leading arguments for that thesis are unpersuasive.

In ordinary cases, unless a desire of ours is irresistible, it is up to us, in some sense, whether we act on it; and it is widely thought that relatively few desires are irresistible. Arguably, in many situations in which we act against our reasoned better judgments, we could have used our resources for self-control in effectively resisting temptation. (On this issue, see chapter 5.) Normal agents can influence the strength of their desires in a wide variety of ways. For example, they can refuse to focus their attention on the attractive aspects of a tempting course of action and concentrate instead on what is to be accomplished by acting as they judge best. They can attempt to augment their motivation for performing the action judged best by promising themselves rewards for doing so. They can picture a desired item as something unattractive—for example, a wedge of chocolate pie as a wedge of chewing tobacco—or as something that simply is not arousing. Desires normally do not have immutable strengths, and the plasticity of motivational strength is presupposed by standard conceptions of self-control.

The key to understanding core weak-willed action, in my view, is a proper appreciation of the point that the motivational strength of a motivational attitude does not need to be in line with the agent's evaluation of the object of that attitude. Our reasoned better judgments are based, in significant part, on our assessments of the objects of our desires; and when assessment and motivational strength are not aligned, we may believe it best to *A* and better to *A* than to *B* while being more strongly motivated to *B* than to *A*. If while we continue to have that belief (a belief based on practical reasoning), we freely and sanely *B* in the absence of depression, *B* is a core weak-willed action.

6. Delay of Gratification: Some Studies

Walter Mischel and colleagues have produced a fascinating body of work on delay of gratification in children. In *Irrationality* (1987), I use some of that work in developing a theory about how weak-willed actions may be produced. The relatively early work that I discuss there continues to be reviewed in scientific publications (Mischel and Ayduk 2004; also see Holton 2009, pp. 125–27), and I review it myself again here.[12]

In 1970, Mischel and Ebbe Ebbesen reported the results of a study designed to test the hypothesis that "conditions in which [a] delayed reward was present and visually available would enhance attention to it and hence increase voluntary delay time for it" (1970, p. 331). However, the enhanced attention had the opposite effect. Preschool subjects were informed that they would receive a particular preferred reward (cookies or pretzels) if they waited for the experimenter to return and that if they signaled him to return, they would receive instead a particular inferior reward. When both rewards were present during the delay period, mean delay time was 1.03 minutes. When both rewards were absent, there was a mean delay of 11.29 minutes before the children signaled the experimenter to return. Two additional conditions were also tested: when only the preferred reward was present, mean delay time was 4.87 minutes; and when the inferior reward alone was available for attention, the mean delay was 5.72 minutes. Mischel and Ebbesen suggested, plausibly, that "the presence of the rewards serves to increase the magnitude of the frustration effect and hence decreases delay of gratification by making the waiting period more difficult" (p. 337). Inattention to the rewards, in this experiment, was much more effective in promoting delay of gratification.

A subsequent study (Mischel, Ebbesen, and Zeiss 1972) produced the same results and a new finding. When the rewards were absent and the children were instructed to "think fun" during the delay period, the mean waiting time was 14.48 minutes, compared with 0.78 minute for children instructed to think about the reward objects. (The mean delay for children given no instructions was 12.86 minutes.) Mischel and colleagues were careful to note that one cannot properly generalize from these results "to the role of cognition in forms of self-control other than the delay-of-gratification paradigm" (p. 216). However, a tempting generalization *within* the paradigm must also be resisted—namely, that preschool children who attend in no way to the rewards will delay longer than those who do attend to them, independently of the *manner* of attention.

This generalization is undermined in Mischel and Moore (1973). The experimental design is similar to that of the two earlier studies. The main difference is in the presentational conditions. During the delay period subjects were presented with (1) slide-presented images of the reward objects; (2) slide-presented images of irrelevant reward objects; (3) an illuminated blank screen; or (4) an unilluminated screen. In addition, the four different presentational conditions were studied under two different activity conditions, waiting and working; and the presentations were periodic for some subjects and continuous for others. The results are described in table 4.1.

In each of the four conditions specified at the left of the table, subjects presented with slides of relevant rewards delayed the longest. How can this be squared with the results of the earlier studies? Mischel and Moore offer a plausible answer. Following Berlyne (1960), they distinguish between the "motivational (arousal) function" and the "cue (informative) function" of a stimulus (1973, p. 178). Their proposal has two parts. First, in the earlier experiments, the children viewing the reward objects or thinking about them in their absence were focusing on their arousing qualities (their taste, chewiness, crunchiness, or the like), which increased frustration and made waiting more difficult. Second, children

Table 4.1. Mean Delay Time (in Minutes) for All Groups

Task and imagery schedule	Imagery (slide content)			
	Relevant rewards	Irrelevant rewards	Blank slide	No slide
Wait				
Periodic	9.53	5.91	5.06	8.28
Continuous	9.40	3.98	3.30	7.07
Work				
Periodic	8.83	6.58	5.94	3.33
Continuous	8.65	6.12	4.17	4.14

Adapted from Mischel and Moore 1973, table 1, p. 176. Subjects are not permitted to delay more than ten minutes.

attending to the slides of relevant rewards were attending primarily to their informational qualities—in effect, information about what is to be gained by waiting.

Subsequent studies designed to test this proposal (Mischel and Baker 1975; Moore, Mischel, and Zeiss 1976; Mischel and Moore 1980) provide substantial support. In investigating the influence of "cognitive transformations" on delay of gratification, Mischel and colleagues discovered that children instructed to focus on the "consummatory" or arousing qualities of relevant reward objects delayed for a much shorter period than did children instructed to "transform" the desired pretzels and marshmallows into little brown logs and white clouds. Moreover, subjects who transformed the rewards available to them into nonconsummatory objects delayed much longer than subjects instructed to do this with "irrelevant rewards." Mischel and colleagues attribute the latter result to the tendency of subjects' transformational (nonconsummatory) ideation about relevant rewards to remind them of what is to be gained by waiting without frustrating them by focusing attention on consummatory qualities (Mischel and Baker 1975, p. 259; also see Moore et al. 1976, p. 423). Attention to slides or cognitive transformations of relevant rewards may boost the salience for the children of the fact that they can have their preferred treat if they wait, whereas attention to the reward objects themselves (when looking at them or thinking about them) may make salient the prospect of immediate consumption. Attention of the latter kind may generate affectively charged representations of the reward objects that increase motivation for present consumption. In addition, the combination of the pull toward present consumption and the child's preference for the delayed reward may increase stress (Mischel and Ayduk 2004, p. 112) or what Mischel and Ebbesen refer to as "frustration" in a passage I quoted (1970, p. 337); and there is evidence that as stress increases, self-control becomes more difficult (Mischel and Ayduk 2004, p. 110).

Accounting for Backsliding: Background and More • 81

In subsequent work (Metcalfe and Mischel 1999; Mischel et al. 2003; Mischel and Ayduk 2004), Mischel and colleagues add a layer of theory to accommodate the data reviewed here and additional findings. They postulate a pair of systems: a "cool" system that is "cognitive, complex, slow, and contemplative," and a "hot" system that "enables quick, emotional processing" (Mischel and Ayduk 2004, p. 109). These two systems are associated respectively with nonconsummatory and consummatory thought about reward objects. When children are waiting for pretzel or marshmallow rewards, instructions to think of them as "little, brown logs" or "white, puffy clouds" are expected to generate cool representations of the reward objects, thereby activating the cool system and increasing the likelihood of significant delay, whereas instructions to think about them as "salty and crunchy" or "yummy, and chewy" are expected to produce hot, affectively charged representations, thereby activating the hot system and decreasing the likelihood of significant delay (p. 113).

After reviewing the studies I have been discussing, Mischel and Ayduk write:

> it became clear that delay of gratification depends not on whether or not attention is focused on the objects of desire, but rather on just how they are mentally represented. A focus on their hot features may momentarily increase motivation, but unless it is rapidly cooled by a focus on their cool informative features (e.g., as reminders of what will be obtained later if the contingency is fulfilled) it is likely to become excessively arousing and trigger the "go" response. (2004, p. 114)

The hot system, which is present at birth (and develops over time), is geared to relatively immediate action and is steered by affectively charged representations—for example, representations of the taste of pretzels or beer and the pleasant features of parties (Mischel and Ayduk 2004, p. 109). The cool system, which begins to develop in childhood, is in the business of thoughtful evaluation and planning and is guided by information relevant to the agent's goals (pp. 109–10). Examples of cool representations of an object are representations of its size, shape, and nutritional value (Metcalfe and Mischel 1999, p. 12). Children's representations of the chewiness of a marshmallow will tend to be much more arousing than their representations of its shape, and the same goes for typical college students' representations of various pleasures that a certain party is likely to offer as compared with their representations of the party's location or starting time or of the fact that attending the party will probably hurt their performance on tomorrow's test.

Mischel's two-system approach accommodates a lot of data. For my purposes, his work on the effects of representations of different kinds is especially interesting. I do not place any special weight on the two systems themselves.[13] Possibly, some readers find references to hot and cool representations and systems distracting. So I emphasize the main moral I want to draw: There is good evidence that desire strength is not influenced only by (reasoned or unreasoned) evaluations of what is desired; and the way in which agents represent objects of their desires seems to have a significant effect on desire strength.

7. An Application

I turn from children to adults and from Mischel's delay of gratification paradigm to deliberation now about what to do later. Return to my story about Jack (section 1). During breakfast, he deliberated about whether to stay in and study tonight or go to a party instead. He was focused primarily on assessing the respective merits of the two prospective courses of action. In the end, he judged it best to spend the entire evening studying for tomorrow morning's test and then to get a good night's sleep, and he intended to do that. Shortly after dinner, Jack hears a knock at his door. John appears with a case of their favorite beer and invites Jack to have a beer or two before they head off to the party. Jack tells John that he has made up his mind to study for tomorrow's test and to skip the party, and John chuckles; he thinks Jack is joking.

Can this story coherently end as follows? Jack continues to believe that it would be best to stay in and study even when he decides to have a beer with John and then go to the party. Furthermore, when Jack makes this decision he is aware that it conflicts with his better judgment, and when he leaves for the party he is aware that what he is doing clashes with his better judgment. I return to this question shortly. My question now is this: If this story can coherently end this way, how are Jack's deciding to attend the party and his subsequently attending it to be accounted for?

Given the details of the case, it is plausible that when Jack made his decision to attend the party, he was more strongly motivated to attend it than to do otherwise. How can his motivational condition have had that feature, given that (by hypothesis) he also consciously believed at the time that it would be better to study instead? If our conscious beliefs about what it is best to do were uniformly to determine or express what we are most strongly motivated to do, things would not have turned out as I am imagining they did. But, again, there are grounds for rejecting the idea that the connection between beliefs of the kind at issue—or conscious better judgments, including reasoned ones—and motivation is this tight. Conscious better judgments are often based primarily on our reasonable, cool assessments of the objects of our relevant desires, and nothing ensures that the motivational strength of a desire is always in line with the agent's assessment of the desire's object. The motivational strength of a desire can be affected by "hot" representations of the desired object in ways that it is not affected by "cool" representations of that object. Even while an agent consciously believes that the objects of one collection of desires are better than the objects of another collection of desires, the latter collection may have more motivational strength than the former.

Compare Jack's situation while he was deliberating that morning with his situation after John arrives. On the one hand, cool representations of objects of his pertinent desires are likely to have been more prominent than hot, affectively charged ones in the deliberative process that issued in Jack's considered judgment that morning about what it would be *best* to do. Examples of relevant cool representations are Jack's representations of the value of such things as getting a good grade on tomorrow morning's test, studying for the test, being well rested for the test, and attending tonight's party. On the other hand, hot representations of desired objects—representations of the taste of beer, the fun involved in hanging out with friends, and the like—may play a major role in the process that issues in the decision he makes that evening about what *to* do. When John suggests having a beer or two before going to the party, Jack may evaluate his earlier reasoning and conclusion, and the evaluative process may be dominated by cool representations of the objects of the pertinent desires and issue in a conscious belief that his earlier conclusion was correct: it is best not to go to the party. (One can imagine Jack saying to himself, "After all, the important facts about value have not changed.") Even so, at the same time, hot representations of beer drinking and partying may play a major role in the process that issues in his decision to go to the party. And Jack may execute that decision while conscious of the fact that what he is doing is contrary to his better judgment. In light of his motivational condition when he makes the decision, we expect him to execute it; and as far as I can see, nothing entails that when he executes it he is unaware of a conflict between what he is doing and what he continues to believe it best to do.

In a variant of Jack's story, he changes his mind about what it is best to do after John arrives. I certainly do not dispute that this sort of thing sometimes happens. I have attempted to explain how such changes of mind are produced elsewhere (Mele 1996c). My concern here is with the possibility of core weak-willed actions, not with actions that accord with revised better judgments. I return to the possibility of revised better judgments in section 8.

I asked whether Jack's story can coherently end with a decision and corresponding overt conduct that, as he is aware, clash with his better judgment. I have just sketched a hypothesis about how that can happen. If the hypothesis includes no contradiction, the answer is yes. I see no contradiction here; but critics are free to argue that there is one. If and when such arguments are constructed, they can be assessed.

The hypothesis I sketched features the idea that the strength of a desire is not always in line with the agent's evaluation of the object of the desire and two kinds of representation. How an agent represents a desired item can be influenced by a variety of things, including his beliefs about when the desire can be satisfied. In the morning, Jack knows that his desire to attend the party cannot be satisfied for many hours. In the evening, he knows that it can be satisfied relatively soon. In section 5, I mentioned a connection between increased subjective proximity of potential desire satisfaction and increased desire strength that I will discuss in chapter 5. The connection may often be mediated in human beings by an effect of this increased proximity on attention (Mele 1987, pp. 86–93). As the time for desire satisfaction draws very near, our awareness of that fact may be expected to increase the likelihood, frequency, and salience of hot representations of the desired object. And the motivational effect of these representations might not be matched by any effect they may have on evaluation.

My aim in sketching the hypothesis I sketched was to offer an explanation of how Jack's story might end in a certain way. I am not claiming that the hypothesis tells us everything we may want to know about how that ending comes about; and the discussion of self-control in chapter 5 augments the discussion in this section.

To say that Jack's story can end the way I have argued it can is not yet to say that it can end with a core weak-willed action. That depends on whether the actions at issue are free. In this story about Jack, might he have freely decided to attend the party and freely attended it? As semicompatibilists understand free action (see chapter 3, sections 2 and 3), an affirmative answer to this question does not entail that Jack could have done otherwise at the pertinent times than decide to attend the party and attend it. Many other philosophers would view an affirmative answer as entailing that Jack could have done otherwise.[14] Could he have done otherwise? And could he have successfully exercised self-control so as to bring it about that he did not decide to attend the party or to bring it about that he abandoned his decision to attend the party and stayed home? Self-control is the topic of chapter 5.

8. The Socratic Error Theory

In Plato's *Protagoras*, Socrates offers an account of what, in his view, actually happens in what *appear* to be cases of core weak-willed action: owing to the temporal proximity of anticipated pleasures, people change their minds about what it would be best to do (355d–357d). I believe that this sort of thing happens; and, as I mentioned, I attempt elsewhere to explain how it happens (Mele 1996c; also see Holton 2009, ch. 5). I also believe that it is logically possible that there are no core weak-willed actions and that in every apparent instance of core weak-willed action the agent actually changes his mind about what it is best to do. But I believe as well that it is logically possible that in every apparent instance of core weak-willed human action powerful extraterrestrials take control of the human being and compel conduct. The question whether it is *logically possible* that Socrates is right is about as interesting as the question whether the truth of the alien-control hypothesis is a logical possibility. More interesting is the question whether our evidence (understood broadly to include even purely a priori argumentation) renders it probable or improbable that Socrates is right.

Although Socrates's discussion of the topic at hand is subtle and perceptive, a full-blown examination of it is out of place here. The point I want to make is simple. Socrates contends that "it's not . . . in human nature to be prepared to go for what you think to be bad in preference to what is good" (358d). So he seemingly would claim, for example, that it is not in human nature for Jack to go to a party while he believes that so doing would be, on the whole, worse than staying home and studying instead. However, whether this kind of behavior is open to human beings or not depends partly on how processes that give rise to human better judgments are related to processes that give rise to intentional human actions—an empirical matter. And, as I have explained, there is evidence that processes of these two kinds are so related that action-generating processes can issue in intentional actions that are contrary to the agent's reasoned better judgment even while the conscious judgment persists. Once again, whether such actions are core weak-willed actions depends on their being free actions, an issue to which I return in the following chapter.

Socrates grants that "the majority of people . . . hold that many people who know what is best to do are not willing to do it, though it is in their power, but do something else" (*Protagoras* 352d). So, for someone who wishes to respond specifically to Socrates, there is no point in surveying people about whether, in their opinion, they sometimes perform core weak-willed actions. Socrates apparently believes that many people would say yes; and his position implies that they are mistaken about themselves and that researchers like George Loewenstein who claim that people sometimes "behave contrary to their own long-term self-interest, often with full awareness that they are doing so" (1996, pp. 272–73) are mistaken about people in general.

Even though a Socratic skeptic about core weak-willed actions would not be impressed by self-reports on this topic, I was curious about such reports and I conducted a two-part study. Participants in the first part were forty-nine undergraduates in a basic philosophy class at Florida State University. Weakness of will was not on the course agenda. Participants were presented with the text below and asked to circle their answers on a seven-point scale; the extremes, 1 and 7, were labeled, respectively, "Yes, definitely," and "No, definitely not." The text was intended to provide an informal description of core weak-willed action.

> Have you ever done something even though you believed it would be best—from your own point of view, not necessarily the point of view of your parents or peers—to do something else instead, without being forced to do it? For example, have you ever played video games or gone to a party even though you believed at the time that it would be better to study?

The mean response was overwhelmingly positive: 1.224.

Obviously, I used "without being forced to do it" as a way of getting at free will. In the second part of the study, I took a more direct route. I replaced the text just reproduced from part 1 of the study with the following text:

> Have you ever done something of your own free will even though you believed it would be best—from your own point of view, not necessarily the point of view of your parents or peers—to do something else instead? For example, have you ever played video games or gone to a party of your own free will even though you believed at the time that it would be better to study?

Participants were fifty-one undergraduates in a basic logic class at Florida State University; again weakness of will was not on the course agenda. The results were similar to the results of part 1 of the study: the mean response was 1.9. Although these findings would not impress Socrates, many readers may justifiably regard the results as evidence that they are not alone in viewing themselves as capable of performing core weak-willed actions.

FIVE

• • •

Self-Control

The philosophical project of understanding self-control, construed along broadly Aristotelian lines, has its roots in ancient efforts to explain intentional actions. In *De Motu Animalium* (701a7–8), Aristotle asks: "How does it happen that thinking is sometimes followed by action and sometimes not, sometimes by motion, sometimes not?" A proper answer requires understanding, among other things, how it happens that we sometimes act in accordance with our deliberative better judgments and sometimes fail to do so, pursuing instead courses of action at odds with those judgments.

In sections 1 and 2, I sketch some philosophical and psychiatric background on self-control. In sections 3 and 4, I review some relevant work in social psychology. In section 5, with this background in place, I return to the questions about Jack raised toward the end of chapter 4.

1. Philosophical Background

Aristotle views the self-controlled agent as a person whose "desiring element" is "obedient" to his "reason" or "rational principle," though less obedient than the virtuous person's (*Nicomachean Ethics* 1102b26–28). A human being "is said to have or not to have self-control," Aristotle writes, "according as his reason has or has not the control [*kratein*], on the assumption that this is the man himself" (1168b34–35). Given his contention that "reason more than anything else is man" (1178a7; also see 1166a17, 22–23; 1168b27ff.; and Plato, *Republic* 588b–592b), Aristotle's identification of self-control with control by one's reason is predictable.

On an alternative, holistic view of human beings of the sort I favor (Mele 1987, 1995, 2003), the self of self-control is identified with the whole human being rather than with reason. Even when one's passions and emotions run counter to one's better judgment, they often are not plausibly seen as alien forces. A conception of self-controlled individuals as, roughly, people who characteristically are guided by their better judgments even in the face of strong competing motivation does not commit one to viewing emotion, passion, and the like as having no place in the self of self-control. In some cases, our better judgments may reflect our evaluative ranking of competing *emotions* or *appetites*.

If self-control and weakness of will may be manifested in overt behavior, they also may be involved in some purely mental behavior (Mele 1987, ch. 4, 1995, chs. 5 and 7). People may accept principles concerning the acceptance, rejection, and modification of their beliefs, emotions, values, preferences, or desires. Acceptance of such principles may sometimes take the form of judgments. For example, Ann may judge it best to assess her desires and preferences from an impartial perspective, Bob may judge it best to monitor his values with a view to keeping them in line with those of his spiritual leader, and so on. Relevant mental actions of people who are self-controlled in these spheres will accord with the principles they accept. If, for example, Ann is self-controlled regarding evaluative reasoning about her preferences, she reasons about them impartially.

There is ample evidence that motivation often exerts a biasing influence on what we believe, as in cases of self-deception (Kunda 1999; Mele 2001a). Suppose Ann assents to the principle that it is best not to allow what she wants to be true to determine what she believes is true. She may be in a position to exercise self-control in resisting a natural tendency toward motivationally biased belief. Out of a concern to be an unbiased believer about important issues, Ann may endeavor to scrutinize relevant data in an objective way, seek out the advice of experts, and so on.

It is generally recognized that we have some control over whether particular emotions result in action. However, there is also room for self-control in bringing our emotions themselves into line with relevant better judgments (Mele 1995, ch. 6). We may stem an embarrassing flow of sympathy for a character in a film by reminding ourselves that he is *only* a character. The mother who regards her anger at her child as destructive may dissolve or attenuate it by vividly imagining a cherished moment with the child. The timid employee who believes that he can muster the courage to demand a much-deserved raise only if he becomes angry at his boss may deliberately make himself angry by vividly representing injustices he has suffered at the office. These are instances of *internal* control. Many emotions are subject to *external* control as well—control through one's overt behavior. Ann defeats moderate sadness by calling her brother. Bob overcomes modest fears by visiting his coach for an inspirational talk.

Self-control may be either regional or global, and it comes in degrees (Rorty 1980a). The fact that a scholar exhibits remarkable self-control in adhering to the demanding work schedule that he judges best for himself does not preclude his being weak-willed about eating. He may be self-controlled in one "region" of his life and weak-willed in another. And some self-controlled individuals apparently are more self-controlled than others. Agents who have global self-control—self-control in all regions of their lives—would be particularly remarkable, if, in every region, their self-control considerably exceeded that of most people.

In normal agents, a capacity for self-control is not a mental analogue of brute physical strength. We learn to resist temptation by promising ourselves rewards for doing so, by vividly imagining undesirable effects of reckless conduct, and in countless other ways. Our powers of self-control include a variety of skills—and considerable savvy about which skills to use in particular situations.

What I term *orthodox* exercises of self-control serve the agent's better judgment (Mele 1995, p. 32). As I understand self-control, there are also unorthodox exercises of it (Mele 1987, pp. 54–55, 1995, pp. 60–64). Recall young Bruce (chapter 2, section 1). He has decided to join some friends in breaking into a neighbor's house, even though he judges it best on the whole not to do so. Experiencing considerable trepidation, Bruce tries to steel himself for the deed. He succeeds in mastering his fear, and he proceeds to pick the lock. Seemingly, Bruce exercised self-control in the service of a decision that conflicts with his better judgment.

The existence of unorthodox exercises of self-control does not preclude there being a tight connection between self-control and better judgment (Mele 1995, ch. 4). Donald Davidson argues that any interpretable human agent is largely rational, in the sense that his beliefs, intentions, and the like generally cohere with one another and with his behavior (1985a). If this is true, we should expect this rationality to manifest itself in the purposes people have in exercising self-control. Even if the frequency with which self-controlled agents attempt to exercise self-control in support of their better judgments were not to exceed that of other agents, the former agents, owing to their greater powers of self-control, would tend to succeed more often. To be sure, owing to their greater powers, self-controlled agents may also have a greater rate of success in *unorthodox* exercises of self-control. But given the presumption that every interpretable agent is generally rational in Davidson's sense, interpretable agents who make attempts at self-control will tend to do so much more often in support of their better judgments than in opposition to them. As a little arithmetic would show, greater success in the more limited domain of unorthodox self-control is insufficient to counterbalance the effects of greater powers of self-control in the much broader domain.

Some philosophers understand self-control in such a way that unorthodox exercises of it are conceptually impossible. Edmund Henden contends that self-control can only be exercised in the service of "what one takes oneself to have most reason to do" (2008, pp. 73–74, 85). In his view, young Bruce exercises "will-power"—but not self-control—in mastering his fear (p. 85).

Jeanette Kennett contends that what she calls *orthonomous self-control* "best answers to the common-sense notion of self-control" (2001, p. 134). Exercises of orthonomous self-control are restricted to bringing "the agent's actions into line with her view about what is, all things considered, desirable in the circumstances" (p. 133). Thus, in mastering his fear, young Bruce is not exercising orthonomous control.

Whether Kennett is correct in claiming that orthonomous self-control "best answers to *the common-sense notion* of self-control" cannot be settled from the armchair. I conducted a study that featured the following story:

> Fred is an eleven-year-old boy scout. Against his better judgment, he accepted a dare to break into the Smiths' house this evening while they are out. As he approaches their back door that evening, he is frightened and feels very nervous about breaking in, partly because he knows it is wrong to break in. But Fred overcomes his fear and breaks into the house.

Participants were seventy-four undergraduates at Florida State University. They were in the first week of a basic philosophy course, and self-control was not on their course agenda. All participants read this story and then read one or the other of the following two statements:

> A. In overcoming his fear and breaking into the house, Fred displays self-control.
> B. In overcoming his fear and breaking into the house, Fred displays will-power.

They were instructed to indicate whether they agreed or disagreed with the statement (by circling the word "agree" or "disagree.") Participants then turned the sheet of paper over, read the same story, and indicated (in the same way) whether they agreed or disagreed with the other statement. Each statement was on the front side of about half of the questionnaires. There was no significant effect of order. The results are as follows: thirty-four participants (about 46%) agreed that Fred displays self-control, and forty-four participants (about 64%) agreed that Fred displays will-power.

If as Kennett claims, orthonomous self-control "best answers to the common-sense notion of self-control" (2001, p. 134), then nearly half of the participants in this study would seem to have a shaky grip on this notion. Alternative hypotheses include the following two: there is not just one common-sense notion of self-control; there is just one common-sense notion of self-control but it does not strongly favor the verdict that Fred does not display self-control over the contrary verdict. Additional studies may shed further light on common-sense ascriptions of self-control. The study just reported does not inspire confidence in Kennett's claim about the common-sense notion of self-control.

2. Psychiatric Background

Although addicts are often viewed as victims of irresistible desires, this view has met with significant opposition (Bakalar and Grinspoon 1984, Becker and Murphy 1988, Heyman 1996, Peele 1985 and 1989, Szasz 1974). This section explores some theoretical issues surrounding a strategy for self-control of potential use to addicts on the assumption that their pertinent desires *fall short* of irresistibility.

Most desires have more than a momentary existence. If there are irresistible desires, desires that are irresistible at some times may be resistible at others. The guiding assumption of this section has at least two distinct interpretations. In articulating them, some shorthand will prove useful: I use "*a*-desires" as shorthand for "desires characteristic of addicts." On a strong reading, the assumption is that no *a*-desire is irresistible at any time. On a weaker reading, it is assumed that every *a*-desire is resistible at some time or other. Imagine a crack cocaine addict who has exhausted his supply and wants to use more crack as soon as he can. Suppose that, owing partly to this desire, he drives to his brother's house and steals some crack. His driving where he does is motivated by this desire, and the desire is still in place when he steals the drug. On the strong reading of the assumption, this desire is not irresistible even when he gains possession of the drug. On the weak reading, it might be. If the desire is irresistible now, then even though the addict might have been able successfully to exercise self-control in resisting it earlier, there is no longer any chance of that. I leave both readings of the assumption open here.[1]

Work by George Ainslie on self-control and its contrary sheds light on the behavior of addicts and their prospects for self-control, on the assumption just discussed. In early work, Ainslie (1975, 1982) marshals weighty evidence for a view that I summarize in *Irrationality* (1987, p. 85) as follows:

1. "The curve describing the effectiveness of reward as a function of delay is markedly concave upwards" (Ainslie 1982, p. 740). That is, a desire for a "reward" of a prospective action, other things being equal, acquires greater motivational force as the time for the reward's achievement approaches, and after a certain point motivation increases sharply.
2. Human beings are not at the mercy of the effects of the proximity of rewards. They can bring it about that they act for a larger, later reward in preference to a smaller, earlier one by using "precommitting devices," a form of self-control.[2]

These ideas are developed more fully in Ainslie (1992, 2001). Later, I apply them specifically to addiction. A broader focus is useful for introductory purposes.

In Ainslie's view, "personal rules are the most flexible and acceptable precommitting device" (1992, p. 154). He opens a discussion of hyperbolic discount functions and personal rules with the following claim: "It is possible to deduce a mechanism for willpower from the existence of deeply concave discount curves . . . if we assume only that curves from multiple rewards combine in an additive fashion. In brief, choosing rewards in aggregates rather than individually gives later, larger rewards a major advantage over smaller, earlier ones; and the perception of one's current choice as a precedent predicting a whole series of choices leads to just such aggregations" (pp. 144–45).

Consider Beth. She judges it best to adopt a certain exercise routine as a means of losing weight, but she knows that she has a record of violating her exercise resolutions. If Beth has come to believe the following assertion, P, about herself, she might enjoy more success in the future: (P) Whatever choice I make and execute the first time I am tempted to violate my new exercise routine is the choice I will uniformly make and execute on subsequent occasions of temptation. This assertion is not absurd: after all, given that the temptations are similar, how she chooses and acts on the first occasion is evidence about how she will choose and act on relevant subsequent occasions. Given that she believes P, Beth should regard herself now, at time t, as faced with a choice between the following two items: (1) the series of "rewards" to be obtained should she *not* abide by the exercise plan, both on the first occasion of temptation and on all subsequent occasions, and (2) the series of "rewards" to be obtained by *abiding by* this plan on the first and all subsequent occasions of temptation. If, at t, Beth deems the latter series of rewards better, on the whole, than the former, she should choose 2 over 1 (if she can).

Regarding temptation, Ainslie writes: "The crucial time at which preference between . . . two whole series of rewards changes [is the time, t_i] at which the value V' of the series of larger rewards equals the value V of the series of smaller ones," the time of "indifference" (1992, p. 145). "If the choice is made before [t_i], it will favor the series of larger, later rewards, and if it is made after [t_i], it will favor the series of smaller, earlier rewards" (p. 145).

If, at t, Beth chooses the series of "larger, later rewards" to be obtained by abiding by her plan, she thereby adopts a *personal rule* about exercise. "The force of a personal rule," Ainslie writes, "is proportional to the number of delayed rewards that are perceived to be part of the series at risk" (1992, p. 174). "In principle, personal rules make it possible for a person never to prefer small, early alternatives at the expense of the series of larger, later ones. He may be able to keep temptations close at hand without succumbing to them" (p. 193).

As Ainslie sees it, some personal rules are, as I wish to put it, more *self-protective* than others, in virtue of certain properties of the rules themselves. The term "self-protective" should be understood in a double sense: protective of the *rule*, including both its persistence or survival and its not being violated; and protective of the person whose rule it is, or, more precisely, of the person's prospects for maximizing reward. Ainslie summarizes the major self-protective features of rules as follows:

> To be cost-effective, a personal rule must be drawn with three characteristics: (1) The series of rewards to be waited for must be long enough and valuable enough so that it will be preferred over each impulsive alternative. (2) Each member of the series and its impulsive alternatives must be readily identifiable, without ambiguity. (3) The features that exclude a choice from the series must either occur independently of the person's behavior or have such a high intrinsic cost that he will not be motivated to bring them about just for the sake of evading the rule. (1992, p. 162)

Relatively precise rules—rules with "bright lines"—that one has explicitly endorsed (pp. 163–73) are harder to ignore than vague impressions about how one ought to conduct oneself. Rules that one views as serving the maximization of reward, that are precise enough to leave little room for doubt about their application to particular cases, and that are explicitly formulated with a view to excluding the voluntary production of conditions that satisfy the rules' escape clauses, are—in virtue of these very properties—less likely to be violated, other things being equal, than rules lacking one or more of these features.[3] If Ainslie is right, Beth may benefit from adopting an exercise rule with these features.[4]

On Ainslie's view, like Plato's (*Protagoras* 355e–357e), the perceived *proximity* of a reward tends to exert a powerful positive influence on the strength of an agent's motivation to pursue it, an effect that precommitment strategies of self-control, including the tactic of personal rules, are designed to counter. A plausible hypothesis is that, in human beings, this tendency is partly accounted for by an association between increases in perceived proximity and increases in hot representations of the tempting rewards (see chapter 4, section 6). Ainslie contends that "it is in the *addictive* behaviors that the influence of proximity on the temporary preferences is especially evident: For instance, an alcoholic may plan not to drink, succeed if he keeps sufficiently distant from the opportunities, become overwhelmingly tempted when faced with an imminent chance to drink, but later wholeheartedly regret this lapse" (1992, p. 98, my italics). He says, in the same vein, that "the behaviors that seem best to fit the description 'temporarily preferred' are often called addictions. They have a clear phase of conscious though temporary preference, followed by an equally clear period of regret" (p. 97). According to Ainslie, "Acts governed by willpower evidently are both diagnostic and causal. Drinking too much is diagnostic of a condition, alcoholism out of control, but it causes further uncontrolled drinking when the subject, using it to diagnose himself as out of control, is discouraged from trying to will sobriety" (p. 203).

Merely choosing (or deciding, or intending) to refrain from a certain kind of tempting activity indefinitely (for example, cocaine use) is not sufficient for using the tactic of personal rules. To use the tactic, one must view what is to be gained by resisting as a series of rewards stretching out over a considerable time. Ainslie contends that people who take this long view of things will tend to do better at resisting relevant temptations than people who do not; for, other things being equal, the longer the series of similar rewards one has in view, the more strongly motivated one will be to actualize the series.[5] The point about motivation is plausible; how often the resultant motivation will be enough to sustain resistance is an empirical matter.

The success of the tactic of personal rules also depends on how well-tailored one's rules are to oneself. A sedentary, middle-aged man concerned about his deteriorating physical condition might envision a lengthy series of rewards associated with daily exercise. But if he deems it highly unlikely that he would abide by a daily exercise routine, a rule requiring exercise three days a week may prove more beneficial. Given that one's motivation to follow a rule is partly a function of one's subjective probability that one will succeed in following it and achieve the associated rewards, the man may be more motivated to pursue the less demanding routine, even though he believes that the daily routine would yield greater rewards were he to follow it faithfully. Some failures by agents who employ the tactic of personal rules may be attributable, not to any flaw in the tactic itself, but to their setting their sights unrealistically high.

Whether the tactic of personal rules works and how reliably it works are empirical matters, of course. If we can satisfy ourselves, independently of their succeeding in resisting temptation, that a group of people are employing the tactic, we can wait and see how well they fare in resisting temptation.

And we can see how well they fare relative to people who judge it best to resist but do not employ this tactic.

3. Implementation Intentions and Self-Control

I turn to some work in social psychology that bears importantly on self-control. A large body of work on "implementation intentions" provides encouragement concerning our prospects for self-control (for reviews, see Gollwitzer 1999; Gollwitzer and Sheeran 2006). Implementation intentions, as Peter Gollwitzer conceives of them, "are subordinate to goal intentions and specify the when, where, and how of responses leading to goal attainment" (1999, p. 494). They "serve the purpose of promoting the attainment of the goal specified in the goal intention." In forming an implementation intention, "the person commits himself or herself to respond to a certain situation in a certain manner."

In one study of participants "who had reported strong goal intentions to perform a BSE [breast self-examination] during the next month, 100% did so if they had been induced to form additional implementation intentions" (Gollwitzer 1999, p. 496). In a control group of people who also reported strong goal intentions to do this but were not induced to form implementation intentions, only 53% performed a BSE. Participants in the former group were asked to state in writing "where and when" they would perform a BSE during the next month. These statements expressed implementation intentions.

Another study featured the task of "vigorous exercise for 20 minutes during the next week" (Gollwitzer 1999, p. 496). "A motivational intervention that focused on increasing self-efficacy to exercise, the perceived severity of and vulnerability to coronary heart disease, and the expectation that exercise will reduce the risk of coronary heart disease raised compliance from 29% to only 39%." When this intervention was paired with the instruction to form relevant implementation intentions, "the compliance rate rose to 91%."

In a third study reviewed in Gollwitzer (1999), drug addicts who showed symptoms of withdrawal were divided into two groups. "One group was asked in the morning to form the goal intention to write a short curriculum vitae before 5:00 p.m. and to add implementation intentions that specified when and where they would write it" (p. 496). The other participants were asked "to form the same goal intention but with irrelevant implementation intentions (i.e., they were asked to specify when they would eat lunch and where they would sit)." Once again, the results are striking: although none of the people in the second group completed the task, 80% of the people in the first group completed it.

Many studies of this kind are reviewed in Gollwitzer (1999), and Gollwitzer and Paschal Sheeran report that "findings from 94 independent tests showed that implementation intentions had a positive effect of medium-to-large magnitude . . . on goal attainment" (2006, p. 69). Collectively, the results provide evidence that the presence of relevant distal implementation intentions significantly increases the probability that agents will execute associated distal "goal intentions" in a broad range of circumstances. In the experimental studies that Gollwitzer reviews, participants are explicitly asked to form relevant implementation intentions, and the intentions at issue are consciously expressed (1999, p. 501). (It should not be assumed, incidentally, that all members of all of the control groups lack conscious implementation intentions. Indeed, for all anyone knows, most members of the control groups who executed their goal intentions consciously made relevant distal implementation decisions.)

Research on implementation intentions certainly suggests that one useful technique for mastering anticipated motivation not to do what one judges it best to do later—for example, exercise next week or finish writing a c.v. by the end of the day—is simply to decide, shortly after making the judgment, on a very specific plan for so doing. Of course, what works against relatively modest motivational opposition might not work when the opposition is considerably stronger.

4. An Energy Model of Self-Control

Roy Baumeister writes: "If it were up to me to set national policy in psychological matters, I would recommend replacing the cultivation of self-esteem with the cultivation of self-control" (2002, p. 130). "Self-control," as he understands it, "refers... to conscious efforts to alter [one's own] behavior, especially restraining impulses and resisting temptations" (p. 129). Baumeister produces evidence that "self-control operates on the basis of a limited resource, akin to energy or strength, that can become depleted through use" (p. 130). His "energy model" of self-control predicts that "performance at self-control would grow worse during consecutive or continuous efforts, just as a muscle becomes tired" (p. 131).[6]

This prediction of "ego depletion" (Baumeister et al. 1998) has been confirmed. For example, in one study (Muraven et al. 1998), participants who regulated their emotions (either by amplifying or suppressing them) while watching a sad video clip gave up faster in a test of physical stamina than a control group that watched the same clip. In another study (Baumeister et al. 1998), hungry participants instructed to eat radishes rather than tempting chocolates and cookies gave up much faster on a puzzle than people in the control groups. One control group was allowed to eat the tempting desserts, and the other saw no food. "A mere five minutes of resisting the temptation to eat cookies and making oneself eat radishes instead reduced subsequent persistence on difficult puzzles from 21 minutes to 8 minutes" (Baumeister 2002, p. 133).

Ego depletion has been linked to blood glucose. There is considerable evidence that exercises of self-control reduce blood glucose levels (Gailliot et al. 2007). And not only are low levels of blood glucose after a self-control task correlated with poor performance on a second self-control task, but there also is evidence that glucose drinks between self-control tasks attenuate the effect of ego depletion (Gailliot et al. 2007).

Baumeister and his colleagues also tested the hypothesis that our capacity for self-control improves with practice. Participants who exercised self-control in various ways over a two-week period later displayed significantly more self-control than a control group (Muraven et al. 1999). This is encouraging news.

Baumeister reports that "Muraven (1998) . . . showed that the effects of ego depletion could be resisted if the stakes were high enough" (2002, p. 134). A substantial monetary reward for successful performance on the second self-control task results in good performance. After an initial self-control task, "new challenges are apparently evaluated for their importance. If they are not highly important, the self holds back from exerting itself, but when something important does arise, the self is willing to expend more of its remaining resources" (p. 134).[7]

5. Self-Control and "Could Have"

This chapter's discussion of self-control was prompted by some questions about Jack's story that I raised in chapter 4. Despite judging it best to stay in and study, Jack decided to attend the party and then acted accordingly. I asked whether Jack could have successfully exercised self-control to bring it about that he did not decide to attend the party and whether, after he made that decision, he could have successfully exercised self-control to bring it about that he abandoned it and stayed home.

My primary reason for discussing the work highlighted in the preceding three sections is that, along with the work on delay of gratification discussed in chapter 4, it provides readers with an experimentally grounded sense of various factors that influence our conduct in cases of motivational conflict and supports the idea that there is significant behavioral variability in this sphere. For example, low blood glucose levels tend to decrease persistence on tasks that participants have agreed to undertake without ensuring decreased persistence; and higher levels of reward help people persist on such tasks in the presence of low blood glucose without ensuring undiminished persistence. Similarly, although implementation intentions are remarkably effective in promoting achievement of goal intentions, they do not ensure conduct aimed at those goals. And Ainslie's precommitting devices promote—without ensuring—successful resistance of temptation.

In light of the empirical work reviewed here, wouldn't it be surprising if no one like Jack—no one who decided and acted contrary to what he believed at the time to be best—could have exercised self-control to bring it about that he did not so decide or that he acted as he believed best? It might be claimed that if determinism is true, then no one ever could have done otherwise than he or she did. Traditional compatibilists reject this claim, as I have observed (chapter 3, section 3); and, in any case, I am not assuming that determinism is true. Determinism can be set aside here as a potential source of distraction.

In chapter 3, I examined a pair of arguments—arguments A and B—for the thesis that all intentional actions contrary to the agent's better judgment are unfree. The premises of each of those arguments may be used in a corresponding argument for the thesis (*NSC*) that no agent who acts contrary to his conscious better judgment could have exercised self-control to bring it about that he did not so act. I comment briefly on each of the two corresponding arguments.

Here are the first two premises of argument A: (*A1*) Holding at t a judgment that it is best to A at t is conceptually sufficient for intending at t to A at t; and (*A2*) Any agent who intends at a time to A then but does not A then is unable to A at the time. These premises jointly entail the following proposition: ($A3^*$) Any agent who holds at t a judgment that it is best to A at t but does not A at t is unable to A at t. And the conjunction of $A3^*$ and the truism ($A4$) that no agent who, at t, is unable to A at t is able at t to exercise self-control in such a way as to bring it about that he A-s at t entails ($A5$) that any agent who holds at t a judgment that it is best to A at t but does not A then is unable at t to exercise self-control in such a way as to bring it about that he A-s at t. However, the objections I raised to $A1$ and $A2$ in chapter 3 have not disappeared. The argument for *NSC* that I have just formulated is undermined by those objections.

I turn to argument B, the first two premises of which read as follows: ($B1$) An agent's succumbing to a desire contrary to his better judgment cannot be explained by his choosing not to resist, nor by his making a culpably insufficient effort to resist; and ($B2$) Only one explanation remains: the agent was *unable* to resist. The conjunction of $B2$ and the truism ($B3^*$) that no agent who was unable to resist a desire was able to exercise self-control in such a way as to successfully resist that desire entails ($B4$) that no agent who succumbs to a desire contrary to his better judgment was able to exercise self-control in this way. However, the problems I raised for $B2$ have not disappeared.

What else might seem to recommend *NSC*—the thesis that no agent who acts contrary to his conscious better judgment could have exercised self-control to bring it about that he did not so act? In some cases, exercising self-control in support of one's better judgment is unproblematic. Ann thinks that she spends entirely too much time playing solitaire on her office computer and she believes that it would be best, on the whole, not to play the game at work. At the moment, after another bout of game-playing on her office computer, Ann's motivation to bring it about that she no longer plays the game in her office is stronger than her motivation not to bring this about, and she removes the game from her computer. But consider Ian, who is now more strongly motivated to continue watching a golf tournament on television than he is to do anything else now. Even so, he judges it best to turn off the television and get back to work (Mele 1987, pp. 69–72). Is Ian in a position to exercise self-control in support of his better judgment? It may seem that given that his motivation to continue watching golf is stronger than his motivation to get back to work, his motivation *not* to exercise self-control in support of his getting back to work is stronger than his motivation to exercise self-control for that purpose. Accordingly, it may seem that Ian's motivational condition at the time precludes his exercising self-control in support of his better judgment. A proponent of *NSC* may attempt to defend it by arguing for the thesis that the motivational condition that helps explain why an agent acts against his conscious better judgment precludes his attempting to bring it about that he does not so act. Call this *the motivational preclusion thesis*.

I have argued elsewhere that the motivational preclusion thesis is false (Mele 1987, ch. 5, 1995, ch. 3, 2003, ch. 8). Here I briefly sketch a portion of the argument, drawing on Mele (2003). Readers interested in full-blown arguments know where to look.

Sam has judged it best not to eat between meals until he loses ten pounds and he knows that he has lost only five. He opens his refrigerator to get a diet soft drink to sip while watching a late movie on television and spies a large piece of chocolate pie. The sight of the pie elicits a desire to eat the dessert very soon, and this is Sam's strongest relevant desire at the moment. Can Sam exercise self-control in support of his not eating the pie?

Consider a version of the case in which Sam consulted a behavioral therapist about losing weight. The therapist taught him a technique for situations like the present one. Sam was told that when he feels an urge for a snack, he should remind himself of his resolution, slowly and silently count to ten, and then concentrate on the most important reasons for his resolution before making up his mind about whether to eat. His therapist told him that the technique works (when it does) by diminishing the strength of his desire for a snack while increasing the strength of his desire not to eat; he emphasized that a predictable effect of the latter increase is an increase in the strength of Sam's desire to see to it that he does not eat the tempting snack. Suppose that in the present case, when he feels the urge to eat, Sam recalls the therapist's advice. Might he start counting?

A proponent of the motivational preclusion thesis may claim that the answer is *no* because Sam's being more strongly motivated to eat the pie than not to eat it entails his being more strongly motivated *not* to try to change his motivational condition in a way that favors his not eating the pie than to try to do this. This claim about entailment is false, as I have argued elsewhere (Mele 1987, pp. 69–72, 1995, pp. 41–55, 1996b, pp. 57–62, 2003, ch. 8). Consideration of the following case sheds light on the issue.

> Wilma, who suffers from agoraphobia, has been invited to her son's wedding in a church several weeks hence. Her long-standing fear of leaving her home is so strong that were the wedding to be held today, she would remain indoors and forgo attending. Wilma is rightly convinced that unless she attenuates her fear, she will not attend the wedding. And there is a clear sense in which she is now more strongly motivated to remain at home on the wedding day and miss the wedding than to attend it: her current motivational condition is such that, unless it changes in a certain direction, she will [stay home]. . . . Further, Wilma believes that, owing to her motivation to remain in her house indefinitely, she probably will miss the wedding. (Mele 1996b, pp. 55–56)

If, as I believe, intending to *A* is incompatible with believing that one probably will not *A* (Mele 1992a, ch. 8), Wilma is not yet in a position to intend to attend the wedding.

Even so, it certainly is conceivable that, under the conditions described, she does not have an intention to miss the wedding and, indeed, intends to do her best to reduce her fear so that she will be in a position to attend. Furthermore, there is no good reason to hold that because Wilma is now more strongly motivated (in the sense identified) to stay home on the wedding day than to attend the wedding, she also is more strongly motivated to refrain from trying to attenuate her fear than to try to attenuate it. She sees her fear as an obstacle to something she values doing, and the strength of any desire she may have to refrain from trying to attenuate her fear may be far exceeded by the motivational strength of her fear itself and exceeded, as well, by the strength of her desire to try to bring it about that she is in a position to leave her house on the wedding day and attend the wedding.[8]

To be sure, Wilma has a few weeks to adjust her motivational condition whereas Sam may have only a few moments. But just as Wilma may desire more strongly to try to change her motivational condition than to allow it to persist, so may Sam. And just as Wilma may desire more strongly to try to attenuate her fear with a view to bringing it about that she attends the wedding than not to try this, even though her fear currently is stronger than her desire to attend, Sam may desire more strongly to try his therapist's technique with a view to bringing it about that he abides by his resolution than not to try this, even though his desire to eat the pie soon currently is stronger than his desire not to eat it tonight.

Factors that increase or decrease the likelihood that an agent will act contrary to his conscious better judgment also increase or decrease the likelihood that the agent will fail to make a successful effort of self-control in the service of that better judgment. Relevant in both connections are such factors as how the agent is representing his relevant options, the perceived proximity of the rewards of the tempting option, and the agent's blood glucose level. However, such factors may contribute to an agent's being more strongly motivated to eat a snack, for example, than to refrain from eating it, as he judges best, while leaving it open that the agent is more strongly motivated to exercise self-control in the service of his better judgment than to refrain from doing so.

If an agent who acted contrary to his conscious better judgment could have exercised self-control to bring it about that he did not so act, why might he have failed to make a successful exercise of self-control in the service of his better judgment? Three different kinds of scenario should be distinguished. In one kind of scenario, the agent makes no attempt at self-control even though he believes he should. In another, he impulsively acts contrary to his better judgment not only without making an attempt at self-control but also without even thinking about making one. In a third kind of scenario, the agent makes an unsuccessful attempt.

In an ordinary case of the first kind, one simple answer to the present question features the claim that the agent was more strongly motivated at the time to refrain from exercising self-control than to exercise it, even though he judged it best to exercise it. This motivational fact about the agent can be accounted for in ways that are by now familiar. A critic may claim that the motivational fact entails that the agent *could not* have exercised self-control. But the prospects for producing an adequate defense of this claim do not look promising. If the connection between motivational strength and efforts is indeterministic, the motivational fact at issue is compatible with its being the case that the agent could have exercised self-control. And the same is true even if the connection is deterministic, if traditional compatibilists are right.

In a case of the second kind, it may be true that the agent could have considered exercising self-control in support of his better judgment and that if he had considered doing this, he might have successfully exercised self-control. A partial explanation of the agent's failure to exercise self-control features an explanation of his failure to consider exercising it.

In the heat of the moment, his attention may be so focused on the tempting course of action that it does not occur to him to exercise self-control.

In the third kind of scenario, an agent who could have exercised self-control to bring it about that he did not act contrary to his conscious better judgment makes an unsuccessful attempt at self-control. Unsuccessful attempts to do things that we could have done seem to be extremely common. It seems that golfers try and fail to sink even relatively easy putts they could have sunk, professors try and fail to persuade students of points they could have persuaded them of, salespeople try and fail to make sales they could have made, and so on. I do not see why we should expect things to be different in the sphere of self-control. In the spheres of sports, persuasion, and sales, we offer and accept intuitive explanations of failures of the sort at issue—that is, failures in cases in which (we believe) the agents could have succeeded. We might think that Alf would have sunk the putt if he had concentrated a bit harder, that Ann would have persuaded her student if she had given more thought to exactly what puzzled the student, that Amy would have sold the house to Howard if she had placed more emphasis on the virtues of the neighborhood, and that these agents could have done these things. Again, why should things be thought to be different in the sphere of self-control?

Consider the following case:

> John's present Biology 100 lab assignment is to determine what his blood type is by pricking one of his fingers with a needle and examining a sample of his blood under a microscope. Although John does not mind the sight of his own blood, he is averse to drawing blood from himself. John weighs his reasons in favor of carrying out the assignment against his contrary reasons and judges that [it would be best] to prick his finger . . . and he moves the needle toward his finger with the intention of drawing blood. However, as he sees the needle come very close to his skin, he stops. It is

more difficult than he thought to carry through. He decides that if he did not look at the needle, it would be easier to complete the task. And he tries again, this time without looking. But when he feels the needle touch his finger, he stops. (Mele 1987, pp. 34–35)

On his first attempt, John saw no need for an attempt at self-control. On his second attempt, he saw the need and made an unsuccessful effort to sidestep his aversion. Why did the second attempt fail? One relevant factor is the strength of the pertinent aversion. John seems to think that the focus of his attention is a factor, and he might be right. If looking away from the needle is not enough to solve the attentional problem, doing that while also imagining how he will feel if his friends see him chicken out might reduce the salience of the anticipated pain further while boosting the strength of John's motivation to follow through. This strategy for self-control might have worked, and it may be a strategy that John could have employed. In fact, he might try it on his next attempt—and he might succeed.

This section's primary topic has been *NSC*—the thesis that no agent who acts contrary to his conscious better judgment could have exercised self-control to bring it about that he did not so act. The question this thesis directly raises is whether it is sometimes true that an agent who acted contrary to his conscious better judgment could have exercised self-control to bring it about that he did not so act. In the absence of a good reason to believe that the desires on which we act whenever we act contrary to a conscious better judgment are irresistible, an affirmative answer is extremely plausible.

SIX

• • •

Conclusion

E. J. Lemmon writes: "Perhaps acrasia is one of the best examples of a pseudo-problem in philosophical literature: in view of its existence, if you find it a problem you have already made a philosophical mistake" (1962, pp. 144–45). Whether you have made a mistake in finding weak-willed action to be a problem depends on what you think the problem is. If there are weak-willed actions, explaining why they occur is a potential research project. If it is your project and you do not know why they occur, you have a problem. Good research and careful thought might generate a solution to it.

Lemmon remarks on a "philosophical amazement that there should be such a phenomenon as" weak-willed action (1962, p. 144). If his claim is that such amazement can only be produced by a philosophical mistake, I am inclined to agree. (Obviously, amazement that there should be such a thing as weak-willed action is different from puzzlement about how to account for the occurrence of such actions.) If I had to choose just one short description of just one mistake that can lead to the amazement Lemmon mentions, it would be *a radical overestimation of the power of better judgments*. Many different things may contribute to this mistake, including the belief that A-favoring better judgments are or entail intentions to A, a serious overestimation of human rationality, and confusion about what it is to act freely. I have devoted considerable attention to these matters elsewhere (Mele 1987, 1995, ch. 2, 2003, ch. 5), and I revisited some of them in chapters 3 and 4.

Philosophers who undertake the project of accounting for the occurrence of core weak-willed actions may tend to be inclined to argue for the conceptual possibility of such actions before they take up the project itself. After all, claims that weak-willed actions are conceptually impossible and arguments for that thesis are a very salient part of a tradition that dates back to Socrates; and many philosophers are most at home in the sphere of conceptual possibilities and impossibilities. In chapter 3, I rebutted some arguments for the conceptual impossibility of core weak-willed actions; and in *Irrationality* (1987), I did the same with a wider variety of arguments for that thesis. Notice, however, that if it were to be explained why core weak-willed actions actually happen, the conceptual possibility of such actions would be secured in the process. What actually happens is restricted to the sphere of the conceptually possible.

My first three chapters were devoted largely to conceptual matters. In chapter 4, after some additional conceptual work, I turned to an explanatory issue; I sketched a view about how the occurrence of core weak-willed actions may be accounted for *if* they occur. In chapter 5, I developed that view further, attending to the place self-control and failures thereof have in it. I believe that a typical reader who is confident that free actions are commonplace is now in a position to be relatively confident that core weak-willed actions are not only psychologically possible but actual. In the present chapter, I comment briefly on this belief. (I refer readers who contend that no one ever acts freely to Mele 2006a and 2009. These two books tackle, respectively, philosophical and scientific arguments for this contention.)

I do not expect everyone who reads this book to be persuaded of the existence of core weak-willed actions (even if I believe that they *should* be persuaded of it). An important part of this book's argument that there are core weak-willed actions is a defense of a partial (that is, incomplete) theory about why such actions occur. Some relatively basic ingredients of the theory have philosophical opponents. Notable in this connection are a causal theory about how intentional actions are to be explained and a causal account of the connection between better judgments formed on the basis of practical evaluative reasoning and corresponding intentions. I have defended these two ingredients of the theory at some length elsewhere—in their own right, and not simply as elements of a view about weak-willed actions. I judged it best not to do so again here. For support for the former ingredient (which has not been foregrounded in this book, but definitely is in the background) and replies to objections to causal theories of action explanation, see Mele (2003, chs. 2 and 3, 2010a); and for a defense of the latter ingredient, see Mele (1995, ch. 2, 2003, chs. 4 and 5 and pp. 219–24).[1] While I am at it, I should again mention that I develop an account of the motivational strength of desires of a certain important kind in *Motivation and Agency* (2003, ch. 7). One feature of weakness of will that has made the issue fascinating to philosophers is its entanglement with a host of important philosophical issues, including how our intentional actions are to be explained, the power of practical reasoning and practical evaluative judgments, human rationality, and free will. An author might attempt to give each of these issues its due in a book about weakness of will, but then the book would be enormous. Also, at this point in time, I do not have anything major to add to what I have said in other books about these issues.

Some sophomoric mistakes should be mentioned and quickly set aside. Only a radically confused person would claim that it is a *necessary truth* that core weak-willed actions occur. And only a seriously confused person would claim that a conditional that has a statement of our evidence for the occurrence of core weak-willed actions as its antecedent and the assertion that there are core weak-willed actions as its consequent is a necessary truth. A conditional of that kind certainly does not need to be a necessary truth in order for the truth of the antecedent to constitute powerful evidence for the truth of the consequent. Undergraduates sometimes ask for *proof* that there are (core) weak-willed actions. When pressed on what would constitute proof, their responses occasionally suggest that they want evidence of such a kind that, *necessarily*, given that evidence, there are (core) weak-willed actions. When we get that far, I ask whether they have evidence of such a kind that, necessarily, given it, our classroom exists.

It is improbable, of course, that Socrates, Plato, and other eminent philosophers who have argued that there are no core weak-willed actions were led to that conclusion as a consequence of sophomoric philosophical mistakes. These philosophers would not, for example, assume that we are warranted in believing in the existence of core weak-willed actions only if we show that a conditional of the kind I mentioned is a necessary truth. In any case, the leading arguments for the thesis that there are no core weak-willed actions are arguments for the (conceptual or psychological) *impossibility* of such actions (see Mele 1987, chs. 1 and 2).

I have defined *core weak-willed* action as free, sane, intentional action that, as the nondepressed agent consciously recognizes at the time of action, is contrary to his better judgment, a judgment based on practical reasoning. If such action is psychologically possible, then it is conceptually possible. So, is it psychologically possible?

For the purposes of this book, as I have explained (chapter 3), it is fair to assume that free actions are psychologically possible for at least some human beings. The same goes for sane actions, intentional actions, reasoned better judgments, and practical reasoning. Furthermore, as I mentioned in chapter 3, it is plausible that some compulsive hand-washers, compulsive liars, or crack cocaine addicts are occasionally compelled to perform intentional actions that they consciously recognize at the time to be contrary to their reasoned better judgment. The plausibility of this claim entails the plausibility of the further claim that intentional actions that agents consciously recognize to be contrary to their reasoned better judgment are psychologically possible; and, as I observed in chapter 3, some proponents of the view that core weak-willed actions are impossible appeal to the possibility of compelled or unfree actions of the kind at issue. Of course, all the items just mentioned may be psychologically possible for human beings even if core weak-willed actions are not.

One way to approach the question whether core weak-willed actions are psychologically possible is by asking how actions of this kind (if there are any) might be accounted for. I have asked the latter question, and I have offered an answer. At its core, as I have said (chapter 4, section 5), are the following two theses:

> *T1.* Our better judgments normally are based at least partly on our evaluations of objects of our desires (that is, desired items).
>
> *T2.* The motivational strength of our desires does not always match our evaluations of the objects of our desires.

When eliminativism about desires and better judgments is set aside, the psychological possibility for human beings of better judgments based at least partly on their evaluations of the objects of desires they have is very difficult to deny. Drawing partly on empirical work, I have made a case for the truth of *T2*. If *T2* is true, then, of course, mismatches of the kind at issue are psychologically possible for human beings. And my defense of *T2* motivates a more robust statement: (*T2**) Even in the absence of depression and insanity, the motivational strength of our desires does not always match our evaluations of the objects of those desires. If *T1* and *T2** are true, it is not difficult to see how the following are psychologically possible: (*PP1*) sometimes, even in the absence of depression and insanity, although, on the basis of practical reasoning, we consciously judge it best to *A* and better to *A* than to *B*, we are more strongly motivated to *B* than to *A*; (*PP2*) sometimes, on these occasions, we intentionally *B* and we do not *A* (see chapter 4).

The psychological possibility of *PP2* does not suffice for the psychological possibility of core weak-willed actions. The former psychological possibility is compatible with its being the case that on the occasions at issue it is not psychologically possible for us *freely* to B (while consciously recognizing that what we are doing is contrary to our reasoned better judgment). That is why, in chapter 3, I took pains to show that the leading arguments for the thesis that no actions that conflict with our better judgments can be free are far from persuasive (section 1), identified significant problems that any philosopher who endeavors to defend that thesis will encounter (section 2), and sketched some compatibilist and libertarian ways of distinguishing between compelled actions contrary to one's better judgment and weak-willed actions (section 3); and it is why I devoted as much attention as I did to self-control in chapter 5. I am on record as a defender of the view that free actions are psychologically possible for human beings (Mele 1995, 2006a, 2009), and my defense does not discriminate against weak-willed actions. Moreover, as I observed in chapter 3, typical views of free will in both the compatibilist and the libertarian camps allow for free actions contrary to the agent's conscious, reasoned better judgment.

I said that the theory presented in this book about why core weak-willed actions occur is incomplete. I have attempted to explain how it can happen that the motivational strength of a desire is out of line with the agent's evaluation of the desired object. The explanation appealed to empirical work on a pair of issues: the bearing of different kinds of representations of the objects of desires on behavior; and effects of increased subjective proximity of potential desire satisfaction on motivation. Much more can be learned in both connections; and when it is learned, the knowledge can inform a more fully developed theory about how core weak-willed actions are produced. Interesting relevant questions include the following: What processes link increased subjective proximity of potential desire satisfaction to other changes in how the object of the desire is represented (that is, changes other than in representations of this proximity)? What are the various factors that help generate hot—and cool—representations of the objects of desires, and how do they interact? How strong an influence does increased subjective proximity of potential desire satisfaction tend to have on the evaluation of the object of the desire? And how do hot representations of the objects of desires affect evaluations of them? But I believe we know enough to be confident that if there are free actions, there are core weak-willed actions.

In his essay "Of Miracles," David Hume offered the following maxim: "no testimony is sufficient to establish a miracle, unless the testimony be of such a kind that its falsehood would be more miraculous, than the fact, which it endeavors to establish" (1777, 1975, pp. 115–16). Here is a maxim I find plausible: no theory that entails that core weak-willed actions are psychologically impossible for human beings should be accepted unless its falsehood would be more amazing than the occurrence of core weak-willed actions. To the best of my knowledge, I have not encountered a theory that passes this test.

If I am right, we should believe that core weak-willed actions occur, and our theories about the springs of action, the power of better judgments, human agency, human rationality, practical reasoning, and the like should accommodate their occurrence. Why they occur is, to my mind, a much more interesting question than whether they occur. I have never been in a position to have serious doubts about their existence. As we improve our understanding of why core weak-willed actions occur, we will be better equipped to deal with some of the practical problems to which such books as the one I mentioned at the beginning of my first chapter—Alexandra Logue's *Self-Control*—are addressed.

Notes

CHAPTER 1

1. Of course, knowing that it is best to A is distinguishable from believing that it is best to A. Someone who holds that all action contrary to what one knows to be best is unfree may consistently hold that we sometimes freely act contrary to what we believe to be best.

2. A referee recommended that I say how the view presented in this book is linked to what I have to say about weakness of will in Mele 1987. Seeing what failed to persuade some critics whose work I discuss here has enabled me to develop more forcefully some of the basic ideas about weakness of will presented in that book. I also benefit from some relatively recent empirical work and from many additional years of reading, reflecting on, and writing about the philosophy of action. The view presented here is a refined, updated, and augmented version of the view presented in Mele 1987.

3. For other restrictive features of Aristotle's notion of enkrateia, see Charlton 1988, pp. 35–41.

4. On nondeclarative propositions, see Goldman 1970, pp. 102–5; Hare 1972, ch. 3.

5. In chapter 4 (section 3), I sketch a view of practical reasoning that I have attempted to motivate elsewhere.

6. Stephen Kearns asked about an agent who says that even though his A-ing now would be best on the whole, he ought, on the whole, to B now, which he knows is incompatible with his A-ing now. (The "ought" here, by hypothesis, is not a strictly moral one.) The agent B-s—freely, sanely, and so on. If it is conceivable that he believes what he says, the definition of core akratic action that I

offered can be modified to exclude actions performed on the basis of such "ought" beliefs.

CHAPTER 2

1. For some other exceptions, see Bigelow, Dodds, and Pargetter 1990, Hill 1986, Jackson 1984, and McIntyre 2006. Also see Holton 2009, p. 71, n. 2.

2. A modified version of Holton 1999 appears as chapter 4 of Holton 2009. The modifications do not bear on the issues I discuss in this chapter.

3. In some cases of noncore akratic action, as I conceive of it, agents act contrary to better judgments they once held but akratically rejected (see Mele 1996c). On evaluative judgments of other kinds that agents might act contrary to in cases of noncore akratic action, see Mele 1987, p. 6.

4. "Weakness of will" is most naturally used to designate a condition of an agent. One who uses the expression in that way and treats weakness of will as an analogue of akrasia—a certain trait of character (see chapter 1, section 1)—would view the condition as a trait of character. Alternatively, one can understand weakness of will as a condition of an agent that may or may not be a character trait of his. When Holton says such things as that "weakness of will arises . . . when agents are too ready to reconsider their intentions" (1999, p. 242), he seems to be treating "weakness of will" as shorthand for something like "displays of weakness of will." He gives no indication that he believes that what is displayed must be a character trait.

5. For a similar idea about a kind of intention, see Mele 1987, p. 26: "To make an effort of brute resistance in support of one's doing X is to form or retain an intention to do X in order to bring it about that, rather than succumbing to temptation, one X-s."

6. Some readers may be curious about how other students responded. Four mentioned not standing up for what one believes (or for one's convictions or beliefs). I did not include them in the knowledge/belief group of eleven because it was not clear that the beliefs they had in mind were specifically about prospective actions (as opposed to something more general: e.g., the belief that tolerance is good). Nine mentioned doing something that one does not

"want" to do—for example, having sexual intercourse with one's boyfriend when one does not want to. Several others offered examples such as eating junk food or not exercising, without saying whether the agents were acting contrary to an intention (or resolution, choice, etc.) or to what they knew or believed they should not do. A few students mentioned being ineffective in getting others to do what one wants them to do. Several offered answers of the sort one sees when a student taking a test draws a blank—for example, "People are always willing but fear constitutes the capacity of will"; and "Outside of human thought, the concepts of will and weakness probably have no true meaning. That being said, the notion of a 'weakness of will' seems absurd. I realize that this is my opinion."

7. For an analogous point about an action that is both akratic and enkratic, see Mele 1995, p. 63.

8. Joshua May and Richard Holton report the results of a study of Christabel's story in which, against her better judgment (but not her resolution), she executes her plan to start an affair. Half of the respondents say that she "displays weakness of will in having the affair," 33% disagree, and 17% give a neutral answer (May and Holton n.d., pp. 8–9).

9. In a survey study, May and Holton n.d. found the highest "weakness of will" rating when both features are present.

10. The simplified story reads as follows: "Joe believes that it would be best to quit smoking cigarettes. He is thinking again—this time on New Year's Eve—about when to quit. He knows that quitting will be hard and unless he picks a good time to start he will fail. Joe judges that it would be best to smoke his last cigarette tonight and to be smoke free from then on. When he reports this to Jill, his wife, she asks whether this is his New Year's resolution. He says, 'Not yet. I haven't yet actually decided to quit. Making that decision will be hard. To make it, I'll really have to psych myself up. I've been smoking for forty years. I believe I can quit, but I would definitely miss smoking.' In the end, Joe fails to decide to quit smoking. Tomorrow, he smokes less than usual, but he has his first cigarette minutes after he awakes, as always. However, he could have decided to quit, and if he had he would have quit."

11. I also conducted a study (3a) that differed from study 3 in just one way: the assertion the students were asked to respond to was "Joe does not display any weakness of will in this story." The

mean response to this assertion was 4.54 (that is, about midway between modest disagreement and neutrality). Fifteen of the twenty-six students (about 58%) disagreed with the statement, and ten (about 38%) agreed with it. The difference in outcomes is disconcerting, given that disagreeing with the negative statement—"Joe does not display any weakness of will . . ."—is equivalent to agreeing with the positive counterpart statement. (This is part of what motivated study 4, to be reported shortly.) Even so, the majority of students in both groups (80% in study 3 and 58% in this study) expressed the opinion that Joe displayed some weakness of will.

12. Holton reports that "it is not obvious whether" his account of weakness of will "would classify compulsives as weak willed" (1999, p. 261)

13. This seems to be conceded in May and Holton n.d. There they provide evidence that "the ordinary notion of weakness of will [resembles] a prototype or cluster concept" (p. 2) that includes both akratic actions that violate better judgments without violating resolutions and (in my terminology) unorthodox akratic actions. I take no stand on the precise nature of "the ordinary notion of weakness of will." Nor am I committed to there being exactly one ordinary notion of weakness of will. There is evidence of two or more folk notions or conceptions of intentional action (see Cushman and Mele 2008). Further investigation might turn up something similar in the sphere of weakness of will.

CHAPTER 3

1. For relatively recent worries about this, see Buss 1997, Tenenbaum 1999, and Wallace 1999.

2. Readers will have noticed that this definition substitutes "weak-willed" for "akratic" in the definiendum of a definition stated in chapter 1. In light of the discussion in chapter 2, I regard the substitution as permissible.

3. Compatibilist discussions of compulsion versus causation include Audi 1993, ch. 7; Ayer 1954; Grünbaum 1971; Mill 1979, ch. 26, esp. pp. 464–67; and Schlick 1962, ch. 7. Also see Hume's remarks on the liberty of spontaneity versus the liberty of indifference (1739, bk. II, pt. III, sec. 2). "Compulsion" is sometimes used to

mean "irresistible impulse." If an agent can be compelled to *A* by something other than an irresistible impulse, and independently of having such an impulse, then the compulsion of actions in the sense of "compulsion" operative in this book need not always involve compulsions in the other sense.

4. See Ayer 1954; Bergmann 1977, pp. 234–35; Nowell-Smith 1948; and Smart 1961. Also see Hume 1739, bk. II, pt. III, sec. 2 and Hume 1777, sec. 8. For more recent worries about indeterministic luck, see van Inwagen 2000 and Mele 2006a and 2007.

5. Suppose that a person's being convinced that he cannot do otherwise than X precludes his engaging in practical reasoning about whether to X. Then a compulsive liar who is convinced that he cannot do otherwise than lie to Lisa soon cannot engage in practical reasoning about whether to lie to her soon and therefore cannot judge it best not to lie to her soon on the basis of such reasoning. However, it is implausible that all compulsive liars are always in this condition before they lie. And even someone who believes that his lying sooner or later is inevitable may believe that he can refrain from lying on a particular occasion. Such a person may engage in practical reasoning about, for example, whether to lie to his mother about what he did yesterday, in the belief that he can refrain from lying to her about this; and that belief may be false.

6. This argument is similar to an argument R. M. Hare advances for the impossibility of weak-willed action (1963, ch. 5). I evaluate Hare's argument in Mele 1995, pp. 20–23.

7. Arguably, intentionally "not ordering the salad" is not an action (see Mele 2003, pp. 146–54).

8. Regarding my story about Mike the tourist, David Wall writes (2009, p. 76, n. 12): "Mele's response to [the pertinent claim] by Watson is unsatisfactory. Mele claims that we can coherently imagine a case in which the agent judges *A* to be only slightly better than *B* and so decides not to exercise self-control but to indulge himself and do *B* instead (1987, p. 28). As Tenenbaum (1999) argues this response is silent about cases in which the agent judges *A* to be considerably better than *B* yet still does *B*. Such cases are possible and plausibly make up a large proportion of putative cases of akrasia (see Tenenbaum, 1999, pp. 887–90 for an example and discussion). It is not plausible in that kind of case to say that the agent

is indulging himself." This objection—by Wall and Tenenbaum—is seriously off target. My story about Mike is explicitly offered as a counterexample to the claim that "one who chooses not to exercise self-control in support of one's better judgment no longer holds that *judgment*" (Mele 1987, p. 28). The story's succeeding as a counterexample to this claim is obviously utterly compatible with the existence of "cases in which the agent judges A to be considerably better than B yet still does B."

9. This premise has another element, ($B1b$): An agent's succumbing to a desire contrary to his better judgment cannot be explained by his making a culpably insufficient effort to resist. Again, Watson claims that an insufficient effort cannot be explained by a misjudgment of "the amount of effort required," because misjudgment is "a different fault from weakness of will" (p. 338). In Mele 1987 (pp. 25–27), I argue that misjudgment and weakness may be combined in an explanation of an action contrary to one's better judgment.

10. John Stigall suggested the name for this thesis.

11. For references to the literature, see Mele and Robb 1998 and 2003.

12. Around the middle of the twentieth century several compatibilists viewed determinism as a requirement for free action. See the midcentury references in note 4.

13. For a reply, see Fischer and Ravizza 2000, pp. 470–72; and for a rejoinder to that reply, see Mele 2006b. See Fischer 2006 for a reply to the rejoinder.

14. Fischer reports that he is open to refinements of his theory along these lines (2006, p. 328).

CHAPTER 4

1. For discussion of intentions in a similar story, see Mele 1987, pp. 34–44.

2. An exception might have to be made for people who suffer from anarchic hand syndrome (Marchetti and Della Salla 1998). Such a person might attempt to button his shirt with one hand while attempting to prevent the shirt from being buttoned with the other hand. Sean Spence and Chris Frith suggest that people with this syndrome "have conscious 'intentions to act' [that] are thwarted

by . . . 'intentions' to which the patient does not experience conscious access" (1999, p. 24). Alex does not have this problem.

3. On various interpretations of Aristotle's notion of choice, see Mele 1984, pp. 152–55.

4. For a view that is similar in some respects, see Michael Bratman's discussion (1979) of what he calls "evaluative practical reasoning" (p. 156).

5. On a drawback of exerting energy for purposes of self-control, see the discussion of ego depletion in chapter 5, section 4.

6. Some of this literature is discussed in section 6 and chapter 5. For more on intentions by default, see Mele 1992a, ch. 12.

7. For an informative discussion of how the lines are to be drawn, see Toates 1986, ch. 2. For a statement of a popular view in motivational psychology, see Mook 1987, pp. 104–5.

8. John Atkinson articulates an alleged connection between motivational strength and behavior: "The act which is performed among a set of alternatives is the act for which the resultant motivation is most positive. The magnitude of response and the persistence of behavior are functions of the strength of motivation to perform the act relative to the strength of motivation to perform competing acts" (1957, p. 361). Compare this with a thesis advanced by Davidson: "If an agent wants to do x more than he wants to do y and he believes himself free to do either x or y, then he will intentionally do x if he does either x or y intentionally" (1980, p. 23). For criticism of Davidson's thesis and a defense of an alternative, see Mele 1992a, ch. 3, and 2003, ch. 7.

9. Claim 6 does not assert that every intentional action is a motivated action. It takes no stand, for instance, on whether certain unwanted actional side-effects of intentional actions are themselves intentional actions. For example, when Ann jogs she knowingly shortens the life of her running shoes while having no desire to do that. Claim 6 is silent on the question whether she *intentionally* shortens the life of her shoes, but it asserts that some relevant intentional action is motivated at this time: for example, her jogging.

10. Davidson has argued that having beliefs requires possession of the concept of belief (1982). For an instructive reply, see Jeffrey 1985.

11. On flexibility of this kind as a mark of motivation, see Mele 2003, pp. 7–8.

12. The following five paragraphs derive from Mele 1987, pp. 88–90.

13. Dual processing models are receiving considerable attention in psychology and philosophy alike. For a sampling, see Evans and Frankish 2009.

14. The philosophers I have in mind here include many traditional compatibilists and typical libertarians. As I pointed out in Mele 2006a (p. 6), libertarians can claim that an agent freely A-ed at *t* only if, at *t*, he could have done otherwise than A then or claim instead that an agent who could not have done otherwise at *t* than A then may nevertheless freely A at *t*, provided that he earlier performed some relevant free action or actions at a time or times at which he could have done otherwise than perform those actions. Any free A-ings that occur at times at which the past (up to those times) and the laws of nature are consistent with the agent's not A-ing then may be termed *basically free actions*. In principle, libertarians can hold that an agent's basically free actions that are suitably related to his subsequent A-ing confer freedom on his A-ing even though he could not have done otherwise than A then. It is open to libertarians to accept or reject the thesis that the only free actions are what I am calling basically free actions. In any event, the typical core weak-willed actions that typical libertarian conceptions of free action accommodate are *basically* free actions.

CHAPTER 5

1. Notice that even the weaker reading is fairly strong. Consider a crack addict's desire to use some crack *now*, a desire he just acquired. If that desire is resistible at some time, the relevant time is now. Incidentally, even the much less demanding assumption that *some* desires characteristic of addicts are resistible suffices for present purposes.

2. For further discussion, see Mele 1987, pp. 84–86, 90–93, and 1992a, ch. 4. Also see Elster 1984 on imperfect rationality and precommitment.

3. I set aside the technical question what, exactly, would count as violating (or not violating) a vague or ambiguous rule.

4. An additional alleged feature of personal rules is that behavior guided by them tends to increase the probability that the agent's relevant subsequent behavior will also be guided by them.

5. Among the relevant "other things" are subjective probabilities. In some cases, a lengthening of a series might include a significant decrease in one's subjective probability of achieving its rewards and a net decrease in motivation. For some people, a New Year's resolution (personal rule) like "Don't eat between meals this month" might be more effective in the long run than a resolution *never* again to eat between meals. A person who succeeds for a whole month in this endeavor might then be in a much better position consistently to abide by the latter personal rule.

6. For a philosophical discussion of self-control that benefits from Baumeister's work, see Holton 2003.

7. For some evidence that implementation intentions can counteract ego-depletion, see Webb and Sheeran 2003.

8. For support, see Mele 1996b, pp. 58–62.

CHAPTER 6

1. My defense of the latter ingredient—a causal account of the connection between better judgments formed on the basis of practical evaluative reasoning and corresponding intentions—may be of interest to readers who worry that the account of practical reasoning sketched in chapter 4 does not do justice to the normative authority of better judgments.

References

Ainslie, George. 1975. "Specious Reward: A Behavioral Theory of Impulsiveness and Impulse Control." *Psychological Bulletin* 82: 463–96.

———. 1982. "A Behavioral Economic Approach to the Defense Mechanisms: Freud's Energy Theory Revisited." *Social Science Information* 21: 735–80.

———. 1992. *Picoeconomics*. Cambridge: Cambridge University Press.

———. 2001. *Breakdown of Will*. Cambridge: Cambridge University Press.

Alston, William. 1977. "Self-Intervention and the Structure of Motivation." In T. Mischel, ed., *The Self: Psychological and Philosophical Issues*. Oxford: Blackwell, 399–409.

Aristotle. 1915a. *De Motu Animalium*. Vol. 5 of W. Ross, ed., *The Works of Aristotle*. London: Oxford University Press.

———. 1915b. *Nicomachean Ethics*. Vol. 9 of W. Ross, ed., *The Works of Aristotle*. London: Oxford University Press.

Atkinson, John. 1957. "Motivational Determinants of Risk-Taking Behavior." *Psychological Review* 64: 359–72.

Audi, Robert. 1979. "Weakness of Will and Practical Judgment." *Noûs* 13: 173–96.

———. 1993. *Action, Intention, and Reason*. Ithaca, N.Y.: Cornell University Press.

Ayer, Alfred. 1954. "Freedom and Necessity." In A. Ayer, *Philosophical Essays*. London: Macmillan, 271–84.

Bakalar, James and L. Grinspoon. 1984. *Drug Control in a Free Society*. Cambridge: Cambridge University Press.

Baumeister, Roy. 2002. "Ego Depletion and Self-Control Failure: An Energy Model of the Self's Executive Function." *Self and Identity* 1: 129–36.

Baumeister, Roy, E. Bratslavsky, M. Muraven, and D. Tice. 1998. "Ego-Depletion: Is the Active Self a Limited Resource?" *Journal of Personality and Social Psychology* 74: 1252–65.

Becker, Gary and K. Murphy. 1988. "A Theory of Rational Addiction." *Journal of Political Economy* 96: 675–700.

Bergmann, Frithjof. 1977. *On Being Free*. Notre Dame, Ind.: University of Notre Dame Press.

Berlyne, Daniel. 1960. *Conflict, Arousal, and Curiosity*. New York: McGraw-Hill.

Bigelow, John, S. Dodds, and R. Pargetter. 1990. "Temptation and the Will." *American Philosophical Quarterly* 27: 39–49.

Bratman, Michael. 1979. "Practical Reasoning and Weakness of the Will." *Noûs* 13: 153–71.

Buss, Sarah. 1997. "Weakness of Will." *Pacific Philosophical Quarterly* 78: 13–44.

Charlton, William. 1988. *Weakness of Will*. Oxford: Blackwell.

Clarke, Randolph. 1994. "Doing What One Wants Less: A Reappraisal of the Law of Desire." *Pacific Philosophical Quarterly* 75: 1–10.

Cushman, Fiery, and A. Mele. 2008. "Intentional Action: Two-and-a-Half Folk Concepts." In J. Knobe and S. Nichols, eds., *Experimental Philosophy*. New York: Oxford University Press, 171–88.

Davidson, Donald. 1970. "How is Weakness of the Will Possible?" In J. Feinberg, ed., *Moral Concepts*. Oxford: Clarendon Press, 93–113. Reprinted in Davidson 1980.

———. 1980. *Essays on Actions and Events*. Oxford: Clarendon Press.

———. 1982. "Rational Animals." *Dialectica* 36: 318–27.

———. 1985a. "Incoherence and Irrationality." *Dialectica* 39: 345–54.

———. 1985b. "Replies to Essays I–IX." In B. Vermazen and M. Hintikka, eds., *Essays on Davidson*. Oxford: Clarendon Press, 195–229.

Elster, Jon. 1984. *Ulysses and the Sirens*. Cambridge: Cambridge University Press.

Evans, Jonathan, and K. Frankish. 2009. *In Two Minds: Dual Processes and Beyond*. New York: Oxford University Press.

Fischer, John. 1994. *The Metaphysics of Free Will*. Cambridge, Mass.: Blackwell.

———. 2006. "The Free Will Revolution (Continued)." *Journal of Ethics* 10: 315–45.

Fischer, John, and M. Ravizza 1998. *Responsibility and Control: A Theory of Moral Responsibility*. New York: Cambridge University Press.

———. 2000. "Replies." *Philosophy and Phenomenological Research* 61: 467–80.

Frankfurt, Harry. 1969. "Alternate Possibilities and Moral Responsibility." *Journal of Philosophy* 66: 829–39.

Gailliot, Matthew, R. Baumeister, C. N. DeWall, J. Maner, E. A. Plant, D. Tice, L. Brewer, and B. Schmeichel. 2007. "Self-Control Relies on Glucose as a Limited Energy Source: Willpower Is More than a Metaphor." *Journal of Personality and Social Psychology* 92: 325–36.

Goldman, Alvin. 1970. *A Theory of Human Action*. Englewood Cliffs: Prentice-Hall.

Gollwitzer, Peter. 1999. "Implementation Intentions." *American Psychologist* 54: 493–503.

Gollwitzer, Peter, and P. Sheeran. 2006. "Implementation Intentions and Goal Achievement: A Meta-analysis of Effects and Processes." *Advances in Experimental Social Psychology* 38: 69–119.

Gopnik, Alison. 1993. "How We Know Our Minds—The Illusion of 1st-Person Knowledge of Intentionality." *Behavioral and Brain Sciences* 16: 1–14.

Grünbaum, Adolph. 1971. "Free Will and the Laws of Human Behavior." *American Philosophical Quarterly* 8: 299–317.

Hare, Richard. 1963. *Freedom and Reason*. Oxford: Oxford University Press.

———. 1972. *Practical Inferences*. Berkeley: University of California Press.

Henden, Edmund. 2008. "What Is Self-Control?" *Philosophical Psychology* 21: 69–90.

Heyman, Gene. 1996. "Resolving the Contradictions of Addiction." *Behavioral and Brain Sciences* 19: 561–610.

Hill, Thomas. 1986. "Weakness of Will and Character." *Philosophical Topics* 14: 93–115.

Holton, Richard. 1999. "Intention and Weakness of Will." *Journal of Philosophy* 96: 241–62.

———. 2003. "How Is Strength of Will Possible?" In S. Stroud and C. Tappolet, eds., *Weakness of Will and Practical Irrationality*. Oxford: Clarendon Press, 39–67.

———. 2009. *Willing, Wanting, Waiting*. New York: Oxford University Press.

Hume, David. 1739. *A Treatise of Human Nature*. Reprinted in L. Selby-Bigge, ed., *A Treatise of Human Nature*. Oxford: Clarendon Press, 1975.

———. 1777. *An Enquiry Concerning Human Understanding*. Reprinted in L. Selby-Bigge, ed., *Enquiries*, 3rd ed. Oxford: Clarendon Press, 1975.

Jackson, Frank. 1984. "Weakness of Will." *Mind* 93: 1–18.

Jeffrey, Richard. 1985. "Animal Interpretation." In E. LePore and B. McLaughlin, eds., *Actions and Events*. Oxford: Blackwell, 481-87.

Kane, Robert. 1996. *The Significance of Free Will*. New York: Oxford University Press.

Kennett, Jeanette. 2001. *Agency and Responsibility*. Oxford: Oxford University Press.

Kunda, Ziva. 1999. *Social Cognition*. Cambridge, Mass.: MIT Press.

Lemmon, John. 1962. "Moral Dilemmas." *Philosophical Review* 71: 139–58.

Loewenstein, George. 1996. "Out of Control: Visceral Influences on Behavior." *Organizational Behavior and Human Decision Processes* 65: 272–92.

Logue, Alexandra. 1995. *Self-Control: Waiting until Tomorrow for What You Want Today*. Englewood Cliffs, N.J.: Prentice-Hall.

Marchetti, Clelia, and S. Della Salla. 1998. "Disentangling the Alien and Anarchic Hand." *Cognitive Neuropsychiatry* 3:191–207.

May, Josh, and R. Holton. n.d. "What in the World Is Weakness of Will?" *Philosophical Studies* (forthcoming). DOI 10.1007/s11098-010-9651-8.

McIntyre, Alison. 2006. "What Is Wrong with Weakness of Will?" *Journal of Philosophy* 103: 284–311.

Mele, Alfred. 1984. "Aristotle's Wish." *Journal of the History of Philosophy* 22: 139–56.

———. 1987. *Irrationality*. New York: Oxford University Press.

———. 1992a. *Springs of Action*. New York: Oxford University Press.
———. 1992b. "*Akrasia*, Self-Control, and Second-Order Desires." *Noûs* 26: 281–302.
———. 1995. *Autonomous Agents*. New York: Oxford University Press.
———. 1996a. "Internalist Moral Cognitivism and Listlessness." *Ethics* 106: 727–53.
———. 1996b. "Motivation and Intention." *Journal of Philosophical Research* 21: 51–67.
———. 1996c. "Socratic Akratic Action." *Philosophical Papers* 25: 149–59.
———. 2000a. "Deciding to Act." *Philosophical Studies* 100: 81–108.
———. 2000b. "Reactive Attitudes, Reactivity, and Omissions." *Philosophy and Phenomenological Research* 61: 447–52.
———. 2001a. *Self-Deception Unmasked*. Princeton, N.J.: Princeton University Press.
———. 2001b. "Acting Intentionally: Probing Folk Notions." In B. Malle, L. Moses, and D. Baldwin, eds., *Intentions and Intentionality: Foundations of Social Cognition*. Cambridge, Mass.: MIT Press, 27–43.
———. 2002a. "Akratics and Addicts." *American Philosophical Quarterly* 39: 153–67.
———. 2002b. "Autonomy and Akrasia." *Philosophical Explorations* 3: 207–16.
———. 2003. *Motivation and Agency*. New York: Oxford University Press.
———. 2006a. *Free Will and Luck*. New York: Oxford University Press.
———. 2006b. "Fischer and Ravizza on Moral Responsibility." *Journal of Ethics* 10: 283–94.
———. 2007. "*Free Will and Luck*: Reply to Critics." *Philosophical Explorations* 10: 195–210.
———. 2009. *Effective Intentions*. New York: Oxford University Press.
———. 2010a. "Teleological Explanations of Actions: Anticausalism vs. Causalism." In J. Aguilar and A. Buckareff, eds., *Causing Human Action: New Perspectives on the Causal Theory of Action*. Cambridge, Mass.: MIT Press, 183–98.

———. 2010b. "Weakness of Will and *Akrasia*." *Philosophical Studies* 150: 391–404.

———. 2011. "Self-Control in Action." In S. Gallagher, ed., *Oxford Handbook of the Self*. Oxford: Oxford University Press, 465–86.

Mele, Alfred, and D. Robb. 1998. "Rescuing Frankfurt-Style Cases." *Philosophical Review* 107: 97–112.

———. 2003. "BBs, Magnets and Seesaws: The Metaphysics of Frankfurt-Style Cases." In M. McKenna and D. Widerker, eds., *Freedom, Responsibility, and Agency*. Burlington, Vt.: Ashgate, 127–38.

Metcalfe, Janet, and W. Mischel. 1999. "A Hot/Cool-System Analysis of Delay of Gratification: Dynamics of Willpower." *Psychological Review* 106: 3–19.

Mill, John Stuart. 1979. *An Examination of Sir William Hamilton's Philosophy*. J. Robson, ed., Toronto: Routledge and Kegan Paul.

Mischel, Walter, and O. Ayduk. 2004. "Willpower in a Cognitive-Affective Processing System." In R. Baumeister and K. Vohs, eds., *Handbook of Self-Regulation*. New York: Guilford, 99–129.

Mischel, Walter, O. Ayduk, and R. Mendoza-Denton. 2003. "Sustaining Delay of Gratification over Time: A Hot-Cool Systems Perspective." In G. Loewenstein, D. Read, and R. Baumeister, eds., *Time and Decision*: New York: Russell Sage Foundation.

Mischel, Walter, and N. Baker. 1975. "Cognitive Appraisals and Transformations in Delay Behavior." *Journal of Personality and Social Psychology* 31: 254–61.

Mischel, Walter, and E. Ebbesen. 1970. "Attention in Delay of Gratification." *Journal of Personality and Social Psychology* 16: 329–37.

Mischel, Walter, E. Ebbesen, and A. Zeiss. 1972. "Cognitive and Attentional Mechanisms in Delay of Gratification." *Journal of Personality and Social Psychology* 21: 204–18.

Mischel, Walter, and B. Moore. 1973. "Effects of Attention to Symbolically-Presented Rewards on Self-Control." *Journal of Personality and Social Psychology* 28: 172–79.

———. 1980. "The Role of Ideation in Voluntary Delay for Symbolically Presented Rewards." *Cognitive Therapy and Research* 4: 211–21.

Mook, Douglas. 1987. *Motivation: The Organization of Action*. New York: Norton.

Moore, Bert, W. Mischel, and A. Zeiss. 1976. "Comparative Effects of the Reward Stimulus and Its Cognitive Representation in Voluntary Delay." *Journal of Personality and Social Psychology* 34: 419–24.
Muraven, Mark, R. Baumeister, and D. Tice. 1999. "Longitudinal Improvement of Self-Regulation through Practice: Building Self-Control Strength through Repeated Exercise." *Journal of Social Psychology* 139: 446–57.
Muraven, Mark, D. Tice, and R. Baumeister. 1998. "Self-Control as a Limited Resource: Regulatory Depletion Patterns." *Journal of Personality and Social Psychology* 74: 744–89.
Nowell-Smith, Patrick. 1948. "Free Will and Moral Responsibility." *Mind* 57: 45–61.
Peele, Stanton. 1985. *The Meaning of Addiction: Compulsive Experience and Its Interpretation*. Lexington, Mass.: Lexington Books.
———. 1989. *Diseasing of America: Addiction Treatment Out of Control*. Lexington, Mass.: Lexington Books.
Peters, Richard. 1958. *The Concept of Motivation*. London: Routledge and Kegan Paul.
Plato. 1953a. *Laws*. In B. Jowett, trans., *The Dialogues of Plato*. Oxford: Clarendon Press.
———. 1953b. *Republic*. In B. Jowett, trans., *The Dialogues of Plato*. Oxford: Clarendon Press.
———. 1976. *Protagoras*. Trans. C. C. W. Taylor. Oxford: Clarendon Press.
Pugmire, David. 1982. "Motivated Irrationality." *Proceedings of the Aristotelian Society* 56: 179–96.
Rorty, Amelie. 1980a. "Akrasia and Conflict." *Inquiry* 22: 193–212.
———. 1980b. "Where Does the Akratic Break Take Place?" *Australasian Journal of Philosophy* 58: 333–46.
Scanlon, Thomas. 1998. *What We Owe to Each Other*. Cambridge, Mass: Harvard University Press.
Schlick, Moritz. 1962. *Problems of Ethics*. Trans. D. Rynin. New York: Dover.
Smart, J. J. C. 1961. "Free-Will, Praise, and Blame." *Mind* 70: 291–306.
Smith, Michael. 1997. "A Theory of Freedom and Responsibility." In G. Cullity, ed., *Ethics and Practical Reason*. New York: Clarendon Press, 293–319.

———. 2003. "Rational Capacities, Or: How to Distinguish Recklessness, Weakness, and Compulsion." In S. Stroud and C. Tappolet, eds., *Weakness of Will and Practical Irrationality*. Oxford: Clarendon Press, 17–38.

Spence, Sean, and C. Frith. 1999. "Towards a Functional Anatomy of Volition." *Journal of Consciousness Studies* 6: 11–29.

Stroud, Sarah. 2008. "Weakness of Will." *Stanford Encyclopedia of Philosophy*. http://plato.stanford.edu/entries/weakness-will/

Szasz, Thomas. 1974. *The Myth of Mental Illness: Foundations of a Theory of Personal Conduct*. New York: Perennial Library.

Tenenbaum, Sergio. 1999. "The Judgment of a Weak Will." *Philosophy and Phenomenological Research* 59: 875–911.

Toates, Frederick. 1986. *Motivational Systems*. Cambridge: Cambridge University Press.

van Inwagen, Peter. 2000. "Free Will Remains a Mystery." *Philosophical Perspectives* 14: 1–19.

Walker, Arthur. 1989. "The Problem of Weakness of Will." *Noûs* 23: 653–76.

Wall, David. 2009. "Akrasia and Self-Control." *Philosophical Explorations* 12: 69–78.

Wallace, R. Jay. 1999. "Three Conceptions of Rational Agency." *Ethical Theory and Moral Practice* 2: 217–42.

Watson, Gary. 1977. "Skepticism about Weakness of Will." *Philosophical Review* 86: 316–39.

Webb, Thomas, and P. Sheeran. 2003. "Can Implementation Intentions Help to Overcome Ego-Depletion?" *Journal of Experimental Social Psychology* 39: 279–86.

Index

addicts, 30–31, 35–37, 40, 50, 96–103, 118, 130n1
Ainslie, G., 75–76, 97–101, 106
akrasia, 2–4, 11, 21–28, 31, 63, 67–68, 124n4, 127n8
  meaning of 4, 13–15
akratic actions, 2–11, 13–17, 21–32, 123–24n6, 124n3, 125n7, 126n2. *See also* core akratic actions; core weak-willed actions; weak-willed actions
  orthodox and unorthodox, 14–17, 126n13
  strict, 14, 17
akratic agents, 3–4
Aristotle, 3–4, 13, 21, 63, 68, 91–92, 123n3, 129n3
Atkinson, J., 129n8
Audi, R., 25, 39, 126n3
Ayduk, O., 77, 80–81
Ayer, A., 126n3, 127n4

backsliding, ix, 57. *See also* akratic actions; weak-willed actions
Bakalar, J., 96
Baker, N., 80
Baumeister, R., 104–5, 131n6
Becker, G., 96
Bergmann, F., 127n4

Berlyne, D., 79
best, beliefs or judgments about, 3–7, 16–18, 23–31, 36–46, 50–51, 64–68, 73–77, 82–88, 92–93, 106–8, 119
  and envisioned options, 5–6
  and best exclusively, 5–6, 16
  and best inclusively, 6
  and best on the whole, 5–6
  and knowledge of what is best, 1, 25, 123n1
  and negative best judgments, 6
  and possibility, 5
better judgment, 1, 3, 7–8, 18–24, 35, 48, 57–58, 92–96, 131n1
  characterization of, 4–7
  and desires or motivation, 25, 73–77, 83–87, 119–21
  and intentions, 25, 28–30, 36–42, 58–59, 63–68, 117
  power of, 115
better judgment*, 57–60
Bigelow, J., 124n2
Bratman, M., 129n4
Buss, S., 126n1

Charlton, W., 123n3
Clarke, R., 61
commitments, practical, 15–17, 20–21

compatibilism, 33–34, 43–44, 47–49, 52–55, 106, 111, 120, 126n3, 128n12, 130n14. *See also* semicompatibilism
compulsion, 8, 16, 21, 30–38, 42–55, 86, 118–20, 126n12, 126–27n3, 127n5
could have done otherwise, 2, 12, 34, 46–48, 52–54, 76–77, 86, 105–13, 130n14
core akratic actions, 11, 14, 23–25, 31, 123–24n6, 124n3
   and better judgments, 14
   definition of, 8
   and depression, 8–10
   and rationality, 10
   and sanity, 8–9
core weak-willed actions, 11–12, 57–63, 73–77, 85–89, 116, 130n14
   definition of, 33
   and free actions, 33–55, 76, 86–87, 115–21
   psychological possibility of, 62–63, 118–21
   skepticism about, 34–55, 88–89
   sophomoric mistakes about, 117–18
   theses $T1$ and $T2$ about, 73–77, 119–20
Cushman, F., 126n13

Davidson, D., 4–5, 25, 39, 63, 94, 129n8, 129n10
decisions, 7–9, 14–22, 26–27, 39–40, 46–47, 50–51, 83–86, 94, 101–6, 125n10, 127–28n8
   akratic, 16, 21–22
   cognitive, 6–7
   and commitments, 16–17
   and forming intentions, 63
   free, 39–40, 46–47, 54, 86
delay of gratification, 66, 76–82, 105
depression, 1, 5, 8–10
Della Salla, S., 128n2
desires, 18, 48, 60–64, 67, 80–85, 92. *See also* motivation
   and action-desires, 70–71
   attention to, 81–85, 120
   and children, 71–73
   evaluations of, 73–77, 83–85, 92, 119–21
   irresistible, 1, 30–31, 50–52, 76, 96–97, 107, 113, 126–27n3
   kinds of, 70
   and motivation, 68–73
   and proximity, 75, 85–86, 97, 100, 110–11, 120–21
   and representations, 76, 81–85, 100, 120–21
   resistance of, 2–4, 30–31, 38–45, 52, 61, 75–76, 93–94, 97, 101–7, 124n5, 128n9, 130n1
   strength of, 61, 70, 73–77, 82–85, 108–10, 117–21

Ebbesen, E., 77–78, 80
Elster, J., 130n2
enkratic actions, 4, 14, 17, 125n7
   orthodox and unorthodox, 17
enkratic people, 3
Evans, J., 130n13

Fischer, J., 34, 45, 49–51, 128n13, 128n14
Frankfurt, H., 45
Frankfurt-style cases, 45–47, 53

Frankish, K., 130n13
free actions, 1–5, 9–12, 33–55, 76, 86–87, 115–21, 128n12, 130n14; *See also* free will
free will, 2, 9, 33–34, 88–89, 117, 120. *See also* compatibilism, libertarianism, semicompatibilism
Frith, C., 128n2

Gailliot, M., 104–105
Goldman, A., 69, 123n4
Gollwitzer, P., 102–3
Gopnik, A., 72
Grinspoon, L., 96
Grünbaum, A., 126n3

Hare, R., ix, 2, 34, 57, 63, 123n4, 127n6
Henden, E., 95
Heyman, G., 96
Hill, T., 124n1
Holton, R., 2, 11, 13–14, 17–32, 77, 86, 124nn1, 2, and 4, 125nn8 and 9, 126nn12 and 13, 131n6
Hume, D., 121, 126n3, 127n4

implementation intentions, 40, 102–3, 106, 131n7
intentional actions, 10–11, 20, 31, 35, 58–59, 67–68, 71–73, 87, 91, 117, 124n13, 129n9
two perspectives on, 60–64
intentions, 20, 58, 63, 109–10, 117, 124n5, 128–29n2. *See also* implementation intentions
abandonment of, 16
akratic or weak-willed, 16, 25, 39–40, 65–67

and better judgments, 36–42, 58–60, 63–64, 106–7, 115
and practical evaluative reasoning, 64–68
and weakness of will, 17–30, 124n4, 124–25n6
irrationality, 10, 16, 25

Jackson, F., 14, 124n1
Jeffrey, R., 129n10

Kane, R., 48
Kennett, J., 95–96
Kunda, Z., 92

Lemmon, J., 115
libertarianism, 34, 43–44, 47–49, 54–55, 61, 120, 130n14
Loewenstein, G., 87
Logue, A., 1, 121

Marchetti, C., 128n2
May, J., 29, 125nn8 and 9, 126n13
McIntyre, A., 18, 124n1
Metcalfe, J., 81–82
Mill, J., 126n3
Mischel, W., 77–82
Mook, D., 129n7
Moore, B., 78–80
motivation, 16, 63, 68–73, 79–81, 102–6. *See also* desires
and beliefs or judgments, 9–10, 24–25, 83, 92–93
and practical reasoning, 64–68
strength of, 61–62, 70–77, 83–85, 97, 100–101, 107–13, 117–20, 129nn8, 9 and 11, 131n5

Muraven, M., 104–5
Murphy, K., 96

Nowell-Smith, P., 127n4

Peele, S., 96
Peters, R., 68
Plato, 1, 13, 21, 33, 62, 86, 92, 100, 118
pleasure, 3, 71–73, 82, 86
practical evaluative reasoning, 64–68, 117–21, 131n1. *See also* practical reasoning
characterization of, 64
practical reasoning, 24–25, 61, 73–74, 127n5. *See also* practical evaluative reasoning
proximity, 85–86, 97, 100, 110, 120–21
Pugmire, D., 2, 34

rationality, 10, 16, 20, 67, 94, 115–17, 121
Ravizza, M., 45, 49–51, 128n13
representations, 76, 80
cool and hot, 81–85, 100, 120–21
resolutions, 18–19, 22–32, 125nn8 and 10, 126n13
Robb, D., 46–47, 128n11
Rorty, A., 39, 93

sanity, 8–9
Scanlon, T. 71–73
Schlick, M., 126n3
self-control, 12–13, 65–66, 76–80, 91, 116, 120–21, 127–28n8
and addicts, 96–102

and "could have" exercised successfully, 76, 86, 105–13
energy model of, 104–5, 129n5
and implementation intentions, 102–4
and motivational preclusion thesis, 108–13
orthodox and unorthodox exercises of, 15–17, 94–96
orthonomous, 95–96
psychiatric background on, 96–102
and self-controlled people, 3, 92
sphere of, 3–4, 92–93
survey study on, 95–96
self-help, ix, 75
self-indulgence, 3, 26–27, 66, 127–28n8
semicompatibilism, 45, 48, 51–54, 86
Sheeran, P., 131n7
Smart, J., 127n4
Smith, M., 53
Socrates, 1, 33, 62, 86–89, 116–18
Socratic error theory, 86–89
Spence, S., 128n2
strength of will, 3, 15, 21–22, 26–27, 32
Stroud, S., 25
Szasz, T., 96

Tenenbaum, S., 42, 126n1, 127–28n8
Toates, F., 129n7

van Inwagen, P., 34, 48, 127n4

Walker, A., 25
Wall, D., 127–28n8

Wallace, R., 126n1
Watson, G., 2, 34, 38–42, 48, 127n8, 128n9
weakness of will, ix, 7–8, 92, 117, 123n2, 128n9. *See also* akrasia; weak-willed action
  and agoraphobia, 50–52
  and akrasia, 2–4, 11–32
  and compulsion, 30–38, 43–55, 86–87, 118–20, 126n12
  and depression, 1, 5, 8–10, 14, 33, 57, 60, 76–77, 118–19
  and free will, 34, 39–55
  and insanity, 1, 5, 8–9, 60, 119
  meaning of, 2, 4, 13, 124n4
  survey studies on, 13–14, 18–22, 28–30, 88–89, 124–25n6, 125nn8, 9 and 10, 125–26n11, 126n13
weak-willed actions, 1–2, 11–12, 17–18, 22–23, 33. *See also* akratic actions; core akratic actions; core weak-willed actions
Webb, T., 131n7
willpower, 98, 100

www.ingramcontent.com/pod-product-compliance
Ingram Content Group UK Ltd.
Pitfield, Milton Keynes, MK11 3LW, UK
UKHW041418180426
11947UKWH00007B/198